Nigel Cawthorne is the London-based author of over 200 books, including a number of successful true crime and popular history books. His writing has appeared in over 150 publications.

CULTS

NIGEL CAWTHORNE

Quercus

First published in Great Britain in 2019 by

Quercus Editions Ltd
Carmelite House
50 Victoria Embankment
London EC4Y 0DZ

An Hachette UK company

A CIP catalogue record for this book is available
from the British Library

PB ISBN 978 1 52940 166 0
Ebook ISBN 978 1 52940 164 6

10 9 8 7

Typeset by CC Book Production

Printed and bound in Great Britain by Clays Ltd, Elcograf S p A.

To my fiancée, Crystal Nusum,
who was raised a Jehovah's Witness.

CONTENTS

CULTS - INTRODUCTION

I have to declare an interest here. I was educated as a scientist and am, consequently, a rationalist and an atheist. But I was brought up in a moderately religious family, so I understand what comfort a belief in God can bring – especially in the face of the tribulations that enter even the most well-ordered life and the inevitability of suffering and death that we all must face. It lends even the most timid and fearful a little stoicism.

What I do not understand, however, is why anyone would give up the everyday joys and comforts of this life in the hope that something better awaits on the other side of the grave. This book is crammed with examples of people giving up their family and friends, everything they own and their own autonomy for the salvation proffered by a new messiah. Not only do they give up all creature comforts, they also hand over money to fund others' sometimes ostentatious lifestyles. These takers, these cult leaders, demand self-denial, sometimes even total celibacy of their followers, while some at the same time insist on their own freedom to enjoy sex with their followers' spouses and children. Believers are also sometimes expected to kill or die for the cult.

Of course, this is not true for all cults, but there have been a number of examples among the most notorious. Indeed, the *Oxford English Dictionary* offers two definitions. The first is benign: 'A particular form or system of religious worship or veneration, esp. as expressed in ceremony or ritual directed towards a specified figure or object.' The second is more chilling: 'A relatively small group of people having (esp. religious) beliefs or practices regarded by others as strange or sinister, or as exercising excessive control over members.'

Cult members endure these privations because they believe these are the 'end times'. The apocalypse is just around the corner, followed by the Day of Judgement. However, the Christian apocalypse has been expected since shortly after the death of Christ. Predictions of the Islamic apocalypse are slightly younger, while expectations of the Jewish apocalypse go back at least to the Book of Daniel. Other religions have prophesied apocalypses even longer ago than that.

Some cult members in this book work out when they think the apocalypse is going to be and dispose of their earthly possessions in advance, only to be disappointed when their saviour or messiah does not turn up.. Cultists doggedly return to their calculations, spot an error, then come up with a new prediction – only to be disappointed a second time, if not a third, fourth or fifth. Clearly, they can't wait for the fire and brimstone. Aren't things bad enough as it is?

Indeed, if that was not bad enough, cult members continue believing in their self-appointed messiah, even when that person is shown to be a charlatan, a self-serving snake-oil salesman, a sexual predator or even a paedophile. Money, of course, is involved. People value what they pay for. The adage 'if you want to get rich, start a religion' is attributed to L. Ron Hubbard, who founded Scientology. And he knew what he was talking about.

I am not saying that the people – almost always men – who start these cults are cynically exploiting their followers. It may start out that way, but it is pretty clear that when other people start to believe in them, they get convinced of what they are saying themselves. I once knew a woman who started writing an astrology column just for the petty cash it gave her. She made it up. But pretty soon, she began to believe that through reading the movements of the heavens she really could predict the future. It would be cynical of me to add that this did not lead to her make a killing on the stock exchange or the 3.30 at Chepstow.

Some cult leaders genuinely believe in what they are doing from the off. Indeed, they invest a lifetime of study into it. This is not to be dismissed lightly. Nor are their followers simply gullible sheep. One cult member mentioned in this book was a Nobel prize winner. We all love magicians. We want to be a little tricked and bamboozled. When we go to a clothes shop, we want the sales assistant to tell us that whatever we are trying on suits us. The experience of shopping would not be the same without it.

On the bigger questions – life or death, heaven or hell, how to live your life – we also want reassurance. We want someone we respect and look up to tell us that we are right, or even tell us that we are wrong if they offer a way we can get back onto the right track.

Not only do we need the imprimatur of some authority figure; human beings are social animals as well. We need to surround ourselves with people who agree with us. We want our mates to support the same football team, like the same music, watch the same TV shows, follow the same fashions. So it is not surprising that we herd together with the like-minded.

In cults, the members get the added consolation of believing that they are right and everyone else is wrong, that only their cult knows the only truth. It has been guaranteed to them, because their leader has a unique insight, has spent years in tireless study or has a direct line to God. It is even more satisfying to realize that the secrets of a cult are only revealed one stage at a time. Within cults, there are always inner circles of people who are privy to ever-more esoteric knowledge. Once a person is inside a cult, it feels as if all they have to do is stick at it, keep believing, keep paying, and suffering all the privations asked of them: then they will reap the rewards.

There is no point me being smug here, saying that I was educated as a scientist and a rationalist and am therefore immune to any quasi-religious flummery. We all need something to believe in. After losing what faith I had at an early age and discovering no evidence for the existence of God during a long life, I used to tell people smugly that I was a born-again atheist. Then I realized that I wasn't. I was merely a Pagan. Throughout my life I have comforted myself in the worship of Dionysus – the god of wine and creativity – and Aphrodite – the goddess of female beauty and sexual love. What else could a man need? Some well-heeled followers, perhaps.

Nigel Cawthorne
London, March 2019

1

AUM SHINRIKYO – SUPREME TRUTH

Tokyo's Sarin Gas Attack

Tokyo's subway carries nearly nine million passengers a day. On the morning of 20 March 1995, five members of the Aum Shinrikyo 'Supreme Truth' cult got on different trains at the ends of three lines that converged on the Kasumigaseki, the home of Japan's government. At 8.15 a.m., the height of Tokyo's rush hour, they dropped off bags (having pierced them with the sharpened tip of their umbrellas) on their respective trains, leaving the deadly nerve gas Sarin leaking out into the carriages. The cult's leader, Shoko Asahara, aimed to paralyse the Japanese government as a first step in his plan for world domination. He failed, but twelve innocent people died and five thousand others were hospitalized.

Members of Aum Shinrikyo numbered in the tens of thousands worldwide. Their leader was a forty-one-year-old, half-blind, overweight, hippie conman and murderer, who admired Adolf Hitler and believed that he was the reincarnation of Imhotep, the Egyptian architect of the pyramid at Heliopolis. Born Chizuo Matsumoto, he was educated at a school for the blind. Partial sight in his right eye gave him a tremendous advantage over the other pupils there, and he began to bully and extort money from them.

After marrying his wife, Tomoko, in 1978, he used money from his parents-in-law to set up an acupuncture clinic, before he branched out into making quack medicines. He was prosecuted for fraud when a remedy for rheumatism he was pedalling to pensioners proved to be bogus.

Following the New Age fad for mysticism, he joined a cult called Agonshu, which claimed to beam 'healing power' to its followers from its satellite TV station. In 1984 he registered his own cult as Aum Inc. – 'Aum' after the Hindu mantra 'Om'. After a trip to the Himalayas, he told the cult magazine *Twilight Zone* that he could levitate. This was a simple yoga trick, but a photographer managed to take a shot of him in mid-air.

He changed his name to the exotic-sounding Shoko Asahara. Armageddon was coming at the end of the twentieth century, he said, and he had been chosen to lead God's army. In his first book, *Secrets of Developing Your Supernatural Powers*, the 'Venerable Master', as he called himself, claimed he could read minds, take trips into the fourth dimension, develop X-ray vision and levitate.

In his next book, *The Day of Annihilation*, he predicted Japan would re-arm itself in 1992, leading to a third world war and a nuclear holocaust. This, according to Asahara, could be prevented if 'Buddhas' under his instruction took over every country. Even if nuclear annihilation came, the enlightened one would survive and his followers would emerge as a race of superhumans.

Aum Shinrikyo began recruiting across Japan. In an expensive initiation ceremony, the guru said he was injecting 'divine energy' directly into each new recruit's head. Followers were told that cash donations would speed up their spiritual development. Asahara raised yet more money by selling his beard clippings and bathwater to fanatical followers.

In 1988 Aum set up its headquarters in a compound on the slopes of Mount Fuji. Paying through the nose for week-long seminars there, followers slept on the floor. While Asahara dined on the finest foods, his followers ate one bowl of boiled vegetables a day and drank filthy water. Other hypocrisies included the fact that devotees were forbidden to have sex, while Asahara sated his lust by initiating young female followers into the cult by having sex with them.

Recruits were told that the price of 'truth' was to surrender everything they owned. Once inside the cult, they were cut off from the outside world. Given new names and deprived of sleep, they became highly suggestible to orders; and the smallest act of disobedience would be punished with a beating.

Asahara managed to attract scientists into the group who were seeking some spiritual dimension beyond the rigid materialism they had been taught. Indeed, the five perpetrators of the Sarin attack on the subway comprised a surgeon, an electronics engineer and three physics graduates. An astrophysicist and computer programmer in the group developed an electrical cap that gave the wearer an unpleasant electrical shock every few seconds, which was purported to synchronize the wearer's brainwaves with the master's.

Cracks began to show once Taro Maki, the editor of *Sunday Mainichi*, started to run a series of exposés on Asahara and Aum. This investigative journalism led to the *Mainichi*'s offices and the neighbourhood around Maki's home being plastered with fliers defaming him and his family.

When one follower tried to leave the cult, he was dunked in freezing water as a punishment and later died of hypothermia. Another, who expressed misgivings, had their neck broken. A lawyer who took up the case of families that had lost children to the cult was murdered, along with his wife and baby son. Accused of killing them, Asahara said: 'If I was going to kill someone, I would kill Mr Maki.'

In 1990 Asahara and twenty-five of his followers – each adopting his name – ran for parliament. They were trounced at the polls, so Asahara decided to adopt more extreme tactics.

His scientists began cultivating botulism bacteria, a life-threatening toxin. They sprayed it on the parliament building, but its sloppy cultivation had killed the bacteria and the Japanese government fortunately survived unharmed. Aum scientists then turned to the cultivation of anthrax and members were sent to Zaire in Central Africa to collect Ebola bacteria. Meanwhile, Asahara used Aum's thriving Russian offshoot to acquire weapons and military training. Having failed to purchase a nuclear bomb in Russia, members were sent to Australia to mine uranium.

Factories manufacturing small arms and Sarin nerve gas were set up in the sect's Mount Fuji compound. To fund this, Aum opened a chain of computer shops, fast-food restaurants, beauty salons, coffee shops, dating agencies, construction companies and online services, which were run by Aum members who received no wages. These side businesses afforded Asahara a rock-star lifestyle at the same time that maltreated members of the sect died, and their bodies were incinerated or dissolved in acid and flushed down the drain.

Although the Sarin factory was closed down by the end of 1993, the aim to make 70 tons of Sarin – enough to kill millions of people – persisted. Further compounds were set up in other towns in Japan, where dogmatic mantras were played at full blast throughout the factories, and devotees were paraded through the streets in their white robes. When a land dispute sprang up in Matsumoto in 1994, Sarin attacks were made on the judges involved in the case. They survived, but eight bystanders died.

Sarin production had to stop when newspapers reported the chemical had been found in the topsoil around the Mount Fuji compound. In retaliation, Asahara published lists of prominent enemies in its newspaper – including Emperor Akihito, President Clinton and Madonna.

When a deadly earthquake hit Kobe in January 1995, Asahara blamed the US military, alleging the disaster had been 'triggered electromagnetically'. In his book *Disaster Nears for the Land of the Rising Sun*, he said this was the beginning of the end of contemporary Japan. In an unnerving clue as to what was to come, a map of the Tokyo subway was featured on the back of a flier advertising the book.

Fearing the Tokyo Metropolitan Police Force was closing in on them, a truck carrying a laser was sent to attack their headquarters, but the laser was not powerful enough to damage it. A biological attack on the nearby Kasumigaseki Station also failed. But next came the Sarin gas attack.

THE SARIN ATTACK

The first anyone knew of the gas attack was when a passenger pressed the emergency button at Tsukiji, four stops before Kasumigaseki. Three people collapsed on the train, five on the platform. More collapsed on the streets outside.

On the Hibiya Line, there was full-scale panic at the stop before Kasumigaseki. However, despite passengers being evacuated, the train was only halted when it reached Kasumigaseki.

Two members of staff removed a leaking package from the train on the Chiyoda Line. They died. That train was evacuated at the following station. The train on the Marunouchi Line was also allowed to continue after the first victim had been helped off the train. At the next station, the station master removed the package, but the train was allowed to continue. By the time it was stopped, one person in the same carriage that the Sarin had been in was dead and hundreds had been injured by the gas.

Another station master removed the package from the train travelling in the other direction on the Marunouchi Line – but only after it had passed back and forth through Kasumigaseki three times. The subway was eventually closed down at 9.30 a.m., one hour and twenty minutes after the first victims collapsed.

Doctors were baffled by the symptoms of the victims coming into the emergency rooms. It was only over two hours later, when a military doctor recognized the symptoms of nerve gas, that the antidote was finally prescribed.

As the death toll mounted, it became clear that the victims were not the policemen or government officials the cultists had been targeting. They were ordinary commuters. Asahara told the killers that this was not important – that Aum had simply given the dead the opportunity of moving on to a higher spiritual level.

Aum's Mount Fuji compound was raided two days after the gas attack. Soon after dawn 1,000 police officers in riot gear burst into the compound, where they found people incarcerated and starved. Others were too drugged to speak. They discovered malnourished children, many wearing the electrode caps which would supposedly synchronize their brainwaves with Asahara's, and in a basement there were the ashes of numerous murder victims. Moreover, the police estimated that Aum Shinrikyo had made enough Sarin to kill four million people.

Asahara, however, was holed up in a secret hideaway in the compound. He issued fresh threats and cult members were suspected of other attacks, but, once the authorities had built up a cast-iron case against him, he was eventually arrested on 16 May 1995 and charged with twenty-seven counts of murder. Trials dragged on for ten years. Eventually, on 6 July 2018, twenty-three years after the Sarin attack, Asahara and six other cult members were found guilty and hanged.

However, Aum Shinrikyo continued, changing its name to Aleph. The Russian Aum group became known as the Circle of Light, and was banned by the Russian government in 2016 as a terrorist organization. There were raids on Aleph in Japan the following year. In 2019, an alleged sympathizer drove into a crowd celebrating the New Year in Tokyo, injuring eight pedestrians.

2

FREEMASONS

Secrets of the Craft

A lthough Freemasons claim their ancestry dates back to the building of Solomon's Temple in Jerusalem – some even claim that Adam was the first Mason – the cult's origins seem to have been among the guilds of medieval stonemasons. The name 'Freemason' makes its first appearance in the records of the City of London in 1375. Back then, the population was mostly made up of serfs and peasants tied to the land. Masons, on the other hand, were considered a cut above general society as they were free to move from one site to the next. These stone workers would stay at a lodge.

It wasn't just their peripatetic lifestyle that set them apart from the normal populace; their stonemasonry craft stretched back to Ancient Egypt and beyond. As these special skills were their live-lihood, the masons had good reason to keep their techniques to themselves. An untrained man who pretended to know the craft could wreak havoc, so the Masons developed secret passwords, signs and handshakes as a means of identification.

In the seventeenth century the Freemasons began to admit honorary members to their fraternity who had nothing to do with stone working. In 1619 the City of London's Masons Company founded a sister organization called Acception, which admitted 'accepted members' at twice the normal fee. By the turn of the eighteenth century, there were four lodges in London and the movement was growing apace. The Grand Lodge was set up in 1717 as a governing body to supervise the organization's change from a historic craft guild to a broad social movement.

By this time the rites and rituals of the Masons had become regularized. Ceremonies such as initiation took place in a special room in the Masons' Lodge, which was decorated for the purpose. In the anteroom the initiate was instructed to remove his jacket and bare his left breast – presumably to demonstrate that he was not a woman, since women were not usually allowed to join. The candidate then emptied his pockets of money, so that he entered the order poor and penniless. The left leg of his trousers was then rolled up above his knee and his right foot was 'slipshod' – that is, the initiate wore a slipper instead of a shoe.

The initiate was then 'hoodwinked' or blindfolded to remind him that he entered the order in a state of ignorance. A noose was then put around his neck to remind him of the punishment meted out to those who revealed the order's secrets, and he was led into the inner chamber.

At the door, an officer barred his passage by holding a dagger to his chest. The new member's blindfold would be removed to symbolize the transition from darkness into the light, and the initiate lay down inside the symbolic coffin of the Masonic martyr, Hiram Abiff (the architect of King Solomon's Temple who died rather than reveal the order's secrets). Kneeling before the Lodge's master, the initiate swore not to reveal any of the secrets of Masonry. Then he was taught the secret sign, password and handshake known only to members. This initiation ceremony has remained the same until the present day.

Once initiated, the new recruit becomes a first-degree Mason or apprentice. He is given a set of tools, including a chisel representing the gift of learning, a hammer to symbolize the power of conscience and a two-foot-long ruler to demarcate the twenty-four hours in the day. The apprentice also wears a Mason's apron.

After a period of study, the apprentice becomes a second-degree or 'fellow craft' Mason. At this point he is given a plumb-line to symbolize rectitude, a steel square to represent morality and a spirit level to denote equality. When he later becomes a third-degree or master Mason, he receives a trowel, which represents brotherhood, since a trowel is used to apply the cement that holds the blocks of stone together.

In the eighteenth century there was a vogue for the esoteric and at this time the Masons began to 'discover' ties dating back to ancient cults such as the Rosicrucians, the Knights Templar, the Cathars and the Gnostics. Masons discovered links between the way their organization was structured to Pythagoras, the Ancient Greek mathematician, who, after five years of study, allowed his students to join an inner circle whose members were shown the connection between numbers and the mystical meaning of the universe.

A number of fashionable aristocrats were attracted to the Freemasons, including members of the royal family. Since 1737 at least sixteen royal princes have been Masons, four of whom went on to be crowned king. Clergymen, intellectuals and freethinkers joined them too, perhaps because the society's secrecy allowed them to discuss subversive notions behind closed doors.

The thinking and planning behind the French Revolution was thought to have been hatched in France's many lodges. Indeed, revolutionary spirit seemed to run rife through the lodges: George Washington, John Hancock, Benjamin Franklin, Paul Revere and many other key figures in the American Revolution were Masons. General Lafayette, the young French marquis who rallied to the American cause, was also a Mason.

Colonel John McKinstry was an American officer who was captured during the Civil War by Mohawk Indians. They tied him to a tree and were about to burn him alive when he made a secret Masonic sign. One of the Mohawk Indians, Joseph Brant, who had been initiated into the Masons, abruptly put a stop to the execution. Educated in Europe, Brant had been initiated into the Masons, in London and delivered McKinstry to British officers whom he knew to be Masons also. They returned the colonel to an American outpost.

Elsewhere Masonic lodges have been banned as a political threat. In 1738 Pope Clement XII denounced Freemasonry and excommunicated all those initiated into the craft. The papal ban was lifted in 1965.

In the late nineteenth century, a series of books published in France claimed that Freemasonry was a hive of Satanism and debauchery. The Nazis turned against it too, condemning it as part of the world-wide Jewish conspiracy which they perceived. In 1943 French historian Bernard Faÿ helped to produce a propaganda film called *Forces Occultes* which purported to show how the Masons had started the Second World War.

Freemasonry has long been entwined with Italian politics. In the 1980s a mysterious lodge of Freemasons called P-2 – *Propaganda Due* – were accused of acting as a state within a state. Not only were its leaders prominent members of the establishment, but some also had links to organized crime.

While women are not allowed to join the Freemasons, a women's adjunct organization called Adoptive Masonry was set up in France. Marie Antoinette attended Lodge meetings, and later on Napoleon's wife Josephine was enrolled as France's Grand Mistress. In America the Order of the Eastern Star was set up for the female relatives of Freemasons in 1867.

While British Masons still only have three levels of Masonry, American Masons, such as those in the Ancient and Accepted Rite of Masonry, have thirty-three. Some of the highest members within the order have wonderful titles such as Sublime Prince of the Royal Scent, Grand Elected Knight Kabosh and Perfect Master.

Those American members who are at least thirty-second-degree Masons are eligible to join the Ancient Arabic Order of the Nobles of the Mystic Shrine, or the Shriners, an elite Lodge that raises millions of dollars for charity.

As well as America's Founding Fathers and a number of British kings, other famous Masons include the architect Sir Christopher Wren; the composers Mozart, Liszt and Haydn; the writers Voltaire, Goethe, Alexander Pope, Sir Walter Scott, Rudyard Kipling, Robert Burns, Mark Twain and Oscar Wilde; the aviator Charles Lindbergh; the second man to set foot on the moon, Buzz Aldrin; the founder of the Mormons, Joseph Smith; the politicians Winston Churchill and Theodore Roosevelt and also, purportedly, Lenin and the Shah of Iran.

SPIN-OFFS

The Freemasons have spawned a number of spin-off organizations. One of them is Phi Beta Kappa, which was a fraternity founded by Thomas Jefferson and friends at the William and Mary College, in Williamsburg, Virginia, in 1776. Originally organized along Masonic lines, the rites and the secrecy of the organization were dropped in the 1850s and it became an honorary society whose entry depended on scholarship.

Soon after that, the Order of the Illuminati was established in Bavaria by the idealistic law professor Adam Weishaupt in order to oppose the Jesuits, who dominated Bavaria at that time. The order was established in such a way that its higher levels seemed like a natural progression from the already established first three degrees of Freemasonry, and Weishaupt recruited many members from the Masons for the new order.

By 1794 the order had several thousand members in Austria, Switzerland, Bohemia and Hungary. But when Duke Carl Theodor came to power in Bavaria in 1785 he banned both the Freemasons and the Illuminati. His men raided the home of an Illuminati member and seized incriminating documents, many of which were in code.

In 1797 a book called *Proof of a Conspiracy against All*

the Religions and Governments of Europe, Carried On in Secret Meetings of Free Masons, Illuminati, and Reading Societies, Collected from Good Authorities was published. To this day the Illuminati continues to be one of the world's most shadowy secret organizations.

3

THE COOPERITES

Gloriavale Christian Community

The Cooperites took their name from Neville Cooper, an evangelical preacher who founded the Springbank Christian Community in New Zealand in 1969. This became the Gloriavale Christian Community when it expanded and moved to a larger property. Discipline was strict. Women were to obey men and children were savagely beaten if they misbehaved. In 1995 Cooper was jailed for sexual abuse, on the testimony of his son. And in 2017 Cooper's granddaughter spoke out about the living hell she had endured as a member of the cult, leading to further investigation by the authorities.

Neville Cooper began life in Australia. He married his wife, Gloria, when she was just sixteen. It was seemingly a happy marriage. He was a forceful man and she was passive and compliant.

Cooper preached around Australia, calling his mission the 'Voice of Deliverance'. Those who were saved would enjoy everlasting life in heaven, while sinners would suffer eternal damnation in hell. These stern beliefs somehow attracted generous followers. One donated an aeroplane and Cooper became known as the 'Flying Evangelist'.

Gloria was pregnant with the tenth of their sixteen children when, accompanied by her husband and two other missionaries on a trip to Coolangatta, the plane's engine cut out at 1,000 feet.

They crashed into a forested area and the plane was ripped apart, but those on board miraculously survived. However, since no one knew their whereabouts, they had to cope for three days in the wild. With no prospect of rescue, Cooper set out to swim across a saltwater creek. Exhausted, he reached the far shore and fetched help, and later told the Brisbane *Telegraph News Pictorial* that it 'was only God that delivered them from certain death'.

After a successful gospel revival campaign in New Zealand, Cooper and his growing family emigrated there. He set up the Springbank Christian Church near Christchurch. Following the example of the early church outlined in Acts 2:41–7 of the King James Bible (see boxed text at the end of this chapter), the congregation held their money and possessions in common and formed the Springbank Christian Community. They opened a school which concentrated on Bible studies and supported the enterprise by farming and running businesses such as plumbing, drain-laying, gas-fitting, baking, engineering, fixing cars and carpentry.

In 1991 they bought an isolated farm at the foot of the Southern Alps, bordered by the Haupiri River and Lake Haupiri, which they named after the founder's now-late wife. The community there swelled to 500 members and Gloriavale became an economic powerhouse on the West Coast. It had two large dairy farms and a business exporting sphagnum moss. Their deer farm produced venison and velvet, and any wastage was recycled as pet food or fertilizer. The church also ran an airline. This failed, but they maintained the only helicopter-servicing business on the coast.

Cooper changed his name to Hopeful Christian. He preached that people should wear modest clothes and designed a blue uniform for his followers to wear. The women's dresses were ankle-length so that no bare flesh showed and their hair was covered with a white cap. Make-up and jewellery were considered ungodly. Even wedding rings were banned, as Cooper maintained that they derived from a pagan practice.

Women were to aspire only to be home-makers. Abortion and all forms of contraception were banned. While the women had to submit to the men, the men had to submit to the authority of the church. Absolute obedience was demanded from the children. Every day school began with Bible reading and prayers. Pupils were taught that the outside world was evil, and they were being saved from its lusts. Competitive sport was banned, and discipline was maintained by violent and public beatings.

Hopeful Christian's son Phil, however, rebelled against the regime, and he eventually escaped. In his tell-all account, *Sins of the Father*, he said that the use of sexual images and movies was prevalent among the older men of the group, and that he had had to endure watching his wife being fondled by his father, while young girls were told to join community elders in hot tubs.

After Phil fled the compound, he was told by a community elder that he was banned from having any communication with his five children. But he rescued them in a night-time raid. He went back to rescue his wife, but afterwards she returned to the community, saying that only by having one of the children's parents stay at Gloriavale would they later be accepted into heaven.

Another former member, Karen Winder, one of Christian's granddaughters, said that Gloriavale's men are 'groomed' to have sex with underage girls.

'These children are growing up in an environment where sex is celebrated. The leader thinks that thirteen- or fourteen-year-old girls are ready to have babies – there's no child rape going on,' she said. 'A twenty-three-year-old is not necessarily totally culpable for his actions, because he's been groomed for it.'

There were other forms of abuse. When she was fourteen, one girl was locked in a shack in the bush for four weeks for having a relationship with a boy. She was forced to fast when she became overweight.

'My dad used to beat us all the time, for no reason,' she said. 'I never knew why. You'd go home and Dad would be angry and the first thing he'd do was get a stick and start hitting you.'

In 1994 Hopeful Christian was sentenced to six years in prison on eleven charges of indecent assault, but the Court of Appeal quashed the sentences and his convictions and ordered a new trial. At his second trial in December 1995, he was found guilty of three charges of sexual abuse of young community members and spent almost a year in jail.

In 2017 another of Christian's granddaughters, Lilia Tarawa, gave a TED talk about the cult, in which she said that children were married off at ten or twelve. Kids were married to older men and everyone was made to share everything – from meals to prayers to breastfeeding – while brutal corporal punishment was meted out to people who broke rules. She went on to write *Daughter of Gloriavale: My Life in a Religious Cult*. Her insider's view of the cult was also examined in the award-winning TV documentary *Gloriavale*.

Hopeful Christian, who refused to comment on the fresh allegations, died of cancer in 2018 at the age of ninety-two. He was not missed by former member Yvette Olsen, who said that Christian had sexually assaulted her three times when she was nineteen. She called him a 'dirty old man' of 'unbridled lust' and 'lies', with an insistence upon his 'absolute power'.

ACTS OF THE APOSTLES 2:41–7

41 Then they that gladly received his word were baptized: and the same day there were added unto them about three thousand souls.

42 And they continued steadfastly in the apostles' doctrine and fellowship, and in breaking of bread, and in prayers.

43 And fear came upon every soul: and many wonders and signs were done by the apostles.

44 And all that believed were together, and had all things common.

45 And sold their possessions and goods, and parted them to all men, as every man had need.

46 And they, continuing daily with one accord in the temple, and breaking bread from house to house, did eat their meat with gladness and singleness of heart.

47 Praising God, and having favour with all the people. And the Lord added to the church daily such as should be saved.

From the King James Bible

4

THE KNIGHTS TEMPLAR

Warrior Monks

The Knights Templar was a military order founded in the Holy Land during the Crusades. In 1118 the French nobleman Hugues de Payns and seven other veteran crusaders established the Poor Knights of Christ of the Temple of Solomon to protect Christians travelling from Jaffa to Jerusalem, which the crusaders had captured from the Muslims nineteen years before. Payns named the outfit after Jerusalem's Temple of Solomon, where they were first quartered. Two centuries later, the order was closed down and members tortured or burned to death.

The Poor Knights of Christ was one of three military orders, but, unlike like the Knights Hospitaller and the Teutonic Knights, it was a military order from its foundation. Baldwin I, the first King of Jerusalem, gave them the part of his royal palace lying next to the Al-Aqsa Mosque which, after capture by the crusaders, had become known as the 'Temple of Solomon'.

In 1128 Pope Honorius I officially recognized the order, which had now become known as the Knights Templar. The Catholic Church was in favour of the Templars, as the order seemed to provide a way to curb the excesses of the crusaders, who were described by St Bernard of Clairvaux, the head of the Cistercians, as 'rogues and impious men, robbers and committers of sacrilege, murderers, perjurers and adulterers'.

Many of those recruited into the Templars had previously been excommunicated and were absolved of their sins when they entered the order. This led to a later rule that gave Templars immunity from sentences of excommunication handed down by bishops or parish priests.

The Knights Templar had to swear an oath of fraternity, poverty and chastity. At first, they had no distinctive habit and wore old clothes given to them. Later, the knights adopted a white mantel as a symbol of purity, and a red cross was added during the Second Crusade as a symbol of martyrdom. Other ranks wore a black or brown mantel with a red cross.

Unmarried knights were bound by lifelong vows. They were not even allowed to kiss their mothers and, to ensure that there was no sexual contact between members of the order, they had to sleep fully clothed in lighted dormitories.

St Bernard absolved them from the sin of killing, provided they only killed the enemies of the Church. He called them 'Christ's legal executioners'. The Templars took a vow never to retreat, whatever the odds, and gained a reputation for being ferocious in battle. Other orders were not to surrender or leave the battlefield until the Templar flag had fallen.

Like many modern-day cults, members of the Templar were told to cut themselves off from their families and hand over all their worldly goods to the order when they joined. This made the leaders of the Knights Templar immensely rich.

Since the order was founded to aid travellers, a banking system was set up so that funds could be transferred from place to place safely. They also invested in real estate and soon the Templars' distinctive circular churches and their strongly defended fortresses spread across the Mediterranean and further across Europe. Examples include the Temple Church in London's Inns of Court and the Rosslyn Chapel in Scotland, which found fame thanks to its use in the film adaptation of Dan Brown's bestseller *The Da Vinci Code*.

By the end of the thirteenth century, the Crusades were

effectively over. The Muslims had reconquered the Holy Land and the Knights Templar was robbed of its original purpose. This freed the order from the massive cost of maintaining an army in the Middle East and led impoverished European kings to eye the huge wealth of the Templars and turn against them.

The secrecy surrounding the order brought about rumours of idolatry, homosexuality and devil worship. In 1307 Philip IV of France, who was in debt to the Templars' bank, ordered the arrest of the Templars on the grounds of heresy. He then forced Pope Clement V, the first of the popes to be exiled to Avignon, to give him permission to seize the Templars' property. The following year King Edward II of England seized Templar property in the British Isles, and the London Temple, the order's English headquarters, was closed.

The Inquisition then moved on to torture confessions about their practices out of the Templars. The inquisitors began compiling a lurid dossier on the activities of the order, which included homosexuality, urinating on the cross and worshipping Satan in the form of a black cat which they kissed under its tail. According to the Templars' own confessions, they also worshipped a pagan idol called Baphomet, who was a goat endowed with women's breasts and an erect penis. It wore a five-pointed star, or pentagram, around its neck, and oil, said to be rendered from the flesh of dead infants, was said to be massaged into its skin.

In France, thirty-six Templars were tortured and killed and, in 1310, fifty-four were burned at the stake for impiety, blasphemy and sodomy. In 1312 Pope Clement admitted that there was no evidence of heresy in the order, but, nevertheless, Philip of France insisted that the Pope close the order down. The remaining Templars were allowed to join other orders or go free, but the Grand Master of the order, Jacques de Molay, was imprisoned for life on the strength of his confession, despite it having been extracted under torture and later retracted. He cursed King Philip and Pope Clement as he was burned at the stake.

Nearly 700 years later the Vatican released the minutes of the Templars' trials. Among them was a document in which Pope Clement absolved them of heresy.

TEMPLARS TODAY

The Knights Templar still exists in several forms today. In Mexico, there is a 'Knights Templar' drugs cartel. It was headed by Moreno Gonzáles – a.k.a El Chayo (the Rosary) or El Más Loco (the Craziest One) – until he was killed in a gun battle with the Mexican Army in 2014.

Anders Breivik, the far-right terrorist who killed seventy-seven people in Norway in 2011, claimed to have been a member of the Knights Templar, having attended a meeting with other modern-day members in London in 2002. However, the Norwegian authorities concluded that he had acted alone.

A more benign form of the Knights Templar was the Sovereign Order of the Temple of Jerusalem. Founded as L'Ordre du Temple in France in 1705, it claimed to be a continuation of the original twelfth-century Templars' sect, though the modern-day organization says it is only continuing the traditions of hospitality to Christians of the medieval Knights Templar and raising money for charity. It was reconstituted in 1804 and recognized by Napoleon Bonaparte the following year. In 2001 the order was accredited by the United Nations Economic and Social Council as a non-governmental organization and it is an associate member of the International Peace Bureau and an affiliate of the International Centre for Religion and Diplomacy. It has some 5,000 Knights and Dames worldwide.

The Sovereign Order of the Temple in Jerusalem in Florida 'seeks to emulate the chivalric and charity traditions of the original Templars; its members apply themselves energetically and selflessly to Christian charitable endeavours', while the Grand Priory of Knights Templar in England and Wales involves itself in charitable activities.

The United Religious, Military and Masonic Orders of the Temple and of St John of Jerusalem, Palestine, Rhodes and Malta are a branch of the Freemasons. Some lodges claim direct descent from the original Templars.

Other Templar organizations abound on the internet.

5

THE ORDER OF ORIENTAL TEMPLARS

'Do What Thou Wilt'

The *Ordo Templi Orientis* – or the 'Order of the Temple of the East' or 'Order of Oriental Templars' – was founded in Germany along the ideological lines of the Freemasons. The secretive cult's doctrine was based on a mixture of oriental philosophy and the meditative practice of European tantrism. It claimed to possess the key to all Masonic and hermetic secrets, and these mysteries were revealed as you rose through its nine grades. Rituals involved a ceremonial garter, a dagger and a chalice to represent symbolic sexual intercourse, as there was a strong emphasis on sexual magic in the order. In 1912, Aleister Crowley joined. He quickly took over and bent it to his will.

Aleister Crowley was born in 1875 to a family of austere Plymouth Brethren. Early on he rebelled against the strict and joyless sect, taking to drink and drugs, sleeping with his mother's maidservant and even asking for the body of his stillborn sister to experiment on. When he was refused, he went instead to work on a live cat, taking sadistic delight in carrying out tests to see whether it indeed had nine lives. It was Crowley's mother who first called him the 'Beast', after the Beast in the biblical Book of Revelation: a name he readily accepted.

It was at Trinity College, Cambridge, that Crowley began his lifelong study of the occult. At twenty-three, he joined the Hermetic Order of the Golden Dawn. To practise the magic he learned there, he rented Boleskin House on Loch Ness in Scotland where he carried out black magic. The place was said to be cursed. It was later bought by Jimmy Page of Led Zeppelin and in 2015 the house was ravaged by fire. Four years later the shell of the house and the surrounding land was put on the market for more than £500,000.

During his time as a member of the Hermetic Order of the Golden Dawn, Crowley created a ceremony which involved the deflowering of young girls. This resulted in the prosecution of two cult members for rape in 1901. Crowley's bizarre and disruptive behaviour resulted in his expulsion from the order.

In 1903 Crowley married the psychic medium Rose Kelly. On their honeymoon in Cairo, Crowley supposedly conjured up a spirit called Aiwass, who encouraged him to take drugs. Speaking through Rose, the spirit dictated what would become the text of Crowley's most famous book, *Liber AL vel Legis* or *The Book of the Law*. In it he said that Christianity was about to be swept away and replaced by Thelema, a new religious order, of which he would be the Messiah. He grandly dubbed himself the 'Great Beast 666, Prophet of the New Aeon' and Rose became known as his first Scarlet Woman, named after the prostitute in the Book of Revelation. Crowley's message was simple: Satan was not an external force. He was found within the heart of every man and woman. His unlimited power could be released as a result of a person discarding all moral scruples.

The next few years of Crowley's life were led very much in this vein of evil. He and Rose had split up by 1909, after Crowley accused Rose of drinking a bottle of whisky a day. On a mountaintop in Algiers that same year, Crowley had a revelation that sex was linked to magic and persuaded his mistress at the time, Leila Waddell, to have 'the mark of the Beast' tattooed between her breasts.

Back in 1905 Crowley led an expedition up the world's third highest mountain, Kangchenjunga, in the Himalayas. The trip was a disaster. Four people died and, after rumours of cannibalism abounded, Crowley abandoned the expedition and absconded with the sponsors' money.

Soon after this terrible misadventure, Crowley set up his own cult, which he called Argentum Astrum – the Order of the Silver Star. One of his new acolytes, Victor Neuburg, became the centre-piece of Crowley's new occult ceremonies. These usually involved a series of horrifying rituals enacted within the painted shape of a pentacle on the floor. Worshippers danced within it and watched as Neuburg was sodomized, whipped, and had the outline of an inverted cross carved into his chest. Blood was drunk and faeces were eaten. Snakes were released and a frog was baptized 'Jesus of Nazareth', then crucified and stabbed. Plans were made to kidnap, rape and murder a young girl, and then to cut up her body into nine pieces which would be offered up to nine demons.

In 1912 the head of the Order of Oriental Templars in Germany, Freeman Theodor Reuss, visited Crowley in Scotland. He accused Crowley of revealing the cult's secret rituals, but when Crowley managed to convince Reuss that he had stumbled on the rituals by his own devices, Ruess invited him to join the order. Within five years, Crowley had completely taken over the Order of Oriental Templars, which became a vehicle for his Satanism.

'My master is Satan,' said Crowley. 'Resist not evil.'

To escape the interest of the press and impending bankruptcy caused by his cocaine and heroin addiction, Crowley moved to a derelict farmhouse in northern Sicily. In 1920 he converted it into a satanic temple called the Abbey of Thelema and set up home with his mistress, Leah Hirsig, a schoolteacher he had met in New York in 1918. They had a daughter, Poupée, and invited Leah's friend Ninette Shumway to babysit her. Ninette soon became Crowley's second lover.

They painted a circle and a pentagram on the floor of the

central hall and hung obscene and blasphemous paintings on the walls. One showed the Knight Templars' goat-figure, Baphomet – a name that Crowley had taken for himself – sodomizing a man. A whip, an ornamental phallus and a copy of Crowley's book, *The Black Book of Rituals*, sat on the altar. Devotees would come from all over the world to celebrate a Black Mass there. Crowley would eat a communion wafer smeared with Leah's excrement. He would disembowel a live cat, collect its blood and drink it. In one ceremony, Leah had sex with a goat whose throat was cut at the climax of the ritual. Its blood was collected and consumed.

One visitor, the American actress Jane Wolfe, found the farm-house so squalid that she stayed in a tent outside. The artist's model Betty May was also appalled, but her husband Raoul Loveday was seduced by the whole set-up, with fatal conse-quences. He died three months after drinking the blood of a sacrificial cat. The British tabloids had a field day with tales of 'drugs, magic and vile practices'.

Soon afterwards, a child went missing from a nearby village. Crowley was accused of kidnapping and killing the child and, although no charges were brought, within a week the Italian dictator Benito Mussolini ordered Crowley's expulsion from Sicily.

Leah followed Crowley into exile and managed to tolerate his new mistresses until, in 1925, he ran off with another woman. They continued to correspond but, for Leah, eventually sanity prevailed. Somewhat improbably, Leah returned to America in 1930 and went back to school teaching.

Crowley, meanwhile, stayed busy with writing his lurid autobi-ography, *Confessions*, an autobiographical novel called *The Diary of a Drug Fiend* and a number of pornographic works. He also painted, exhibiting his work in Berlin in 1930.

Supported by other Oriental Templar order members in Ger-many, he produced his book *Magick in Theory and Practice*. He spelt magic with a 'k' to distinguish his occult magic from the art of conjuring. In it, Crowley emphasized the importance of animal and even human sacrifice, stating: 'A male child of perfect innocence and high intelligence is the most satisfactory and suitable victim.'

In a footnote, Crowley claimed to have performed such human sacrifices at an average of 150 times a year between 1912 and 1928 – thereby suggesting he had killed over 2,000 children. And he was unrepentant. In a court case in 1934, Crowley was asked: 'Do you believe as a magician in bloody sacrifice?'

He replied: 'Yes.'

'You say for nearly all purposes human sacrifice is best?'

'Yes, it is,' he said.

Clearly no one believed him.

After the publication of *Magick in Theory and Practice*, Crowley subsided into poverty, thanks in part to his addiction to heroin and cocaine. He spent his twilight years in a private hotel called Netherwood, in Hastings. He died in Brighton in 1947 at the age of seventy-two. His body was cremated in a Black Mass, much to the outrage of the good people of Sussex. His ashes were sent to his successor, the head of the Order of Oriental Templars, Karl Germer.

KARL GERMER AND THE ORDER OF ORIENTAL TEMPLARS IN THE USA

Germer was arrested and interned when the Nazis succeeded in stamping out the Order of the Oriental Templars in Germany in 1937. He was later deported to America, where he set up a number of new lodges in California. One of them was the Church of Thelema in Pasadena. It was run by Jack Parsons, who was a rocket scientist who had developed jet-assisted take-off during the Second World War. Earlier on, Parsons had been a disciple of Wilfred Smith, who in the 1930s had held devil-worshipping parties at the OTO's Agape Lodge that had attracted the Hollywood crowd.

In 1946, Parsons attempted to bring the 'Whore of Babylon' down from the astral plane and make it incarnate in the womb of a woman. The experiment took place over the first three days of March. While chanting various incantations, Parsons had sex repeatedly with a willing devotee, while another member of the order, the science-fiction writer L. Ron Hubbard, made notes. Hubbard then ran off with Parsons' girlfriend and $10,000 of his money to start the Church of Scientology.

6

THE ROSICRUCIANS

The Cult of the Rosy Cross

The Rosicrucians owe their existence to an early Protestant pamphlet published in Kassel in Germany in 1614. Titled *The Universal and General Reformation of the Whole Wide World; Together with the Fama Fraternitas of the Laudable Fraternity of the Rosy Cross, Written to All the Learned and the Rulers of Europe*, it purported to be the manifesto of a brotherhood of alchemists. Although they claimed to know how to turn base metal into gold, they were more interested in spreading spiritual and philosophical wisdom. The founder of the cult was said to be one Christian called Rosenkreutz – '*rosenkreutz*' being the German for 'rosy cross'.

The pamphlet said that Rosenkreutz was born in Germany in 1378 to a poor but noble family. They could not afford his upkeep and sent him to a monastery where he learned Latin and Greek. From there a monk took him on a pilgrimage to the Holy Land.

In Damascus, the boy impressed the elders with his medical and healing skills. They taught him science and mathematics. Then they directed him to a city in Arabia called Damcar, which has never been identified and is probably mythical. There he was taught alchemy and other occult secrets.

In Egypt, Rosenkreutz learned natural history and read the

works of Hermes Trismegistus, who fused Greek ideas with those of ancient Egypt to form the *Hermetic Corpus*. He travelled to Morocco, where he learned magic and the Kabbalah (ancient wisdom in the *Torah* or the first five books of the Bible). During the Renaissance, a Florentine mystic named Pico della Mirandola came up with a Christian version of the Kabbalah which stressed the underlying unity of Christianity, Judaism, paganism and Greek thought. By the time the *Fama Fraternitas* was published, the Christian Kabbalah was popular throughout Europe.)

But Christian Rosenkreutz was ahead of his time. He was troubled by what he had learned about magic and the occult, but he realized that he could use it in the service of the Christian faith as the basis of a spiritual renewal.

Back in Europe, however, no one was interested. All they wanted to know about was alchemy, but Rosenkreutz refused to show them how to change base metal into gold. Instead, he decided to write down everything he had learned. He shared the task with seven monks and built a temple to house the fruits of their labours. The brothers then split up to carry the medical knowledge Rosenkreutz had learned to every corner of the earth. They did this in secret, but each year would reassemble at the temple and, before each of them died, they would pass the knowledge on to a worthy successor.

Rosenkreutz himself died in 1484 at the age of 106, according to the *Fama Fraternitas*. Over a hundred years later, in 1604, the brothers, who now included the author of the *Fama Fraternitas*, found a mysterious tomb. Inside it was Rosenkreutz's perfectly preserved corpse. A book in his hand contained all their secret knowledge. It was now time to open up open their ranks.

In 1615, the year after the *Fama Fraternitas* was first published, it was followed up by *The Confessions of the Rosicrucian Fraternity*. The brotherhood were fundamentalist Christians, it said, and it condemned Muhammad and the Pope.

The following year *The Chemical Marriage of Christian Rosen-kreutz* was published as a pamphlet. This is a strange, magical tale about the purported attendance of Rosenkreutz at the wedding of Frederick V of Bohemia and the daughter of James I of England. However authentic these pamphlets and books might have been, they were a gift to conmen. Some charged non-initiates extortionate amounts to join the sect. Others sold 'transformation powder' to make gold. However, the respected German philosopher Michael Maier said that would-be recruits of the Rosicrucian order were secretly observed for five years and, when recruited, they were sworn to secrecy.

When *Fama Fraternitatis* went on sale in Paris, posters went up, promising that the Rosicrucians could bring everyone universal peace and wisdom and everlasting life, though no details were given about how to join the sect. The Catholic church quickly condemned the cult but, in doing so, gave credence to its existence. The Rosicrucians had made a pact with Satan, the Catholic authorities said. After months of uproar, no Rosicrucians appeared and Parisians concluded they had been the victim of a hoax – or perhaps it had been some fiendish Protestant plot. It was noted that the coat of arms of Martin Luther featured a rose and a cross.

In the eighteenth century, a number of rival Rosicrucian societies sprang up, some claiming provenance back to the Pharaohs and beyond. In Breslau, Sigmund Richter wrote elaborated rules and rituals for his German followers. One German lodge (or branch) insisted that members carry a black silken cord, so they could strangle themselves if they felt tempted to divulge the cult's secrets.

In 1743 the Comte de Saint-Germain held the salons of London spellbound. He claimed to be 2,000 years old and was said to be able to produce gold and precious gems at will. Voltaire described him as 'a man who never dies and knows everything'. He apparently died in 1784, but he was seen at the execution of Marie

Antoinette in 1793 and continued to put in alleged appearances until 1820.

In 1782 *The Rosicrucian Unveiled* was published. Its author said that he had spent vast sums of money and years of devoted study climbing the ranks of his lodge only to discover that the master had no divine revelations to offer. This did not put an end to the Rosicrucian craze. Instead, more swindlers took up the lucrative scam. Conmen were soon selling pieces of the 'philosopher's stone' to turn base metal into gold. Others offered membership ... for a price.

Remnants of earlier Rosicrucian lodges were absorbed into the Freemasons. The Freemasons' Rose-Croix Eighteenth Degree which, from around the end of the eighteenth century, operated as an independent order, seems to have incorporated many of the principles of Rosicrucianism.

In 1888 the poet and numerologist the Marquis Stanislas de Guaita set up the Ordre Kabbalistique de la Rose-Croix. It had a Supreme Council of Twelve, but no other members. In 1890 one of the twelve, Joséphin Péladan, peeled off and set up his own rival order, that of the Rose-Croix of the Temple and the Grail. He lectured on mysticism in art and staged occult plays – including two that he claimed were the missing works of the Greek playwright Aeschylus. He also wrote occult books, including *How to Become a Magus* and *How to Become a Fairy*.

In England in 1865, Robert Wentworth Little and a group of fellow Freemasons formed the Societas Rosicruciana in Anglia in association with a German organization. This combined neo-Christian philosophy with mystical beliefs in reincarnation, clairvoyance, alchemy and magic. In the 1870s it had 144 members in England and 500 worldwide, but it floundered when some members became influenced by the new cult of theosophy. In 1887 those members defected to form the Hermetic Order of the Golden Dawn (see Chapter 10).

ROSICRUCIANISM IN THE USA

One group called the Fraternitatis Rosae Crucis, based in Quakertown, Pennsylvania, claimed to date back to 1858, despite not being heard of until 1907 when R. Swinburne Clymer declared himself its chief Magus. That same year, Carl van Grasshof, a member of the Theosophical Society in Los Angeles, converted to Rosicrucianism, changed his name to Max Heindel and wrote *Rosicrucian Cosmo-Conception*. Again in 1907, the Societas Rosicruciana was founded in upstate New York by Sylvester C. Gould.

In 1909 H. Spencer Lewis founded the Ancient and Mystical Order of the Rosae Crucis, while claiming that American Rosicrucianism started in 1693 when a group of German mystics came to Pennsylvania to isolate the elixir of life in Wissahickon Creek. The lodge apparently faltered in 1801; however, Lewis said, Rosicrucianism followed an ancient 108-year cycle of death and rebirth. By 1915 he claimed that the Ancient and Mystical Order of the Rosae Crucis had 300 members.

To show that that the Ancient and Mystical Order of the Rosae Crucis was the one true Rosicrucian order, Lewis put on a demonstration of alchemy before an invited audience that included a journalist from the *New York World*. Instead of secretly observing recruits for five years, he put adverts in the papers to find them. For as little as $5 down, you could learn the secrets of life and join a select group that included the Pharaoh Akhenaten, Jesus, Plato, Aristotle, Cicero, St Thomas Aquinas, Francis Bacon, Benjamin Franklin and Claude Debussy.

Members got a membership card, a secret password, a magazine and diagrams showing secret handshakes. For an extra $2 a month, members got a home-study course. Then you could initiate yourself. All you had to do was trace out a cross on a mirror, say 'Hail, Holy Cross,' and meditate for three minutes. Finally, you had to touch yourself on the forehead and say 'Peace'.

The Ancient and Mystical Order of the Rosy Cross has since moved online, and flourishes to this day. Lectorium Rosicrucian, the International School of the Rosy Cross, has branches in Britain and America. Its founder, J. Leene, has written numerous books including *The Elementary Philosophy of the Modern Rosy Cross*, *The Universal Gnosis*, *The Egyptian Arch-Gnosis* and *The Secrets of the Brotherhood of the Rosy Cross*, under the pseudonym J. van Rijckenborgh.

7

THE CHURCH OF SATAN

The Devil Goes to Hollywood

On 30 April 1966 – *Walpurgisnacht*, Germany's 'Witches Night' – the First Church of Satan was established in San Francisco. Its founder was former circus artist and animal trainer Anton Szandor LaVey. He quit the circus in the early 1960s to work as a conjuror and hypnotist. Slowly his interest in magic grew and he set up a circle of students studying the black arts. His satanic beliefs were very much in the Aleister Crowley mould: 'There is a beast inside man and it must be exercised not exorcised – channelled into ritual hatred,' he said.

LaVey claimed that satanic ages lasted 1,458 years and that the last cycle had started in AD 508. In the latter, God was on top and Satan was cast down. So, according to LaVey's cosmology, the new satanic age began in 1966. LaVey proclaimed 1966 'Year One, *Anno Satanas*'.

LaVey's beliefs caught the mood of the time. To the contemporary hippie generation Christianity had brought about a miserable concoction of self-restraint, self-mortification, self-denial, self-discipline and conformity. Satanism, on the other hand, offered indulgence, vitality and immediate gratification. Sins, LaVey argued, were really virtues when they brought physical and emotional pleasure. Within just five years he garnered 10,000 disciples worldwide and the church was recognized as a bona-fide religion with resulting tax-free status.

The First Church of Satan attracted a lot of devotees in California because of LaVey's unashamed showmanship. He called himself the Black Pope, dressed all in black, shaved his head and grew a goatee beard. The curtains of his home in San Francisco were black and never opened. A human skeleton hung at the end of the hallway. The living room was full of stuffed animals, including a full-grown wolf and a raven. His wife claimed to be a fully fledged witch and her hair hung three feet below her shoulders. He also produced two books: *The Satanic Bible* and *The Satanic Rituals*. These works have been cited at almost as many murder trials as Crowley's *Magick in Theory and Practice*.

LaVey would use a pantomime devil-suit for his ceremonies, complete with horns and a tail, and he would be greeted with the cry: 'Hail, Satan!' His congregation would also be masked and robed in theatrical style. There was obligatory nudity. A naked woman draped across the altar was, of course, *de rigueur*.

LaVey took Satanism to the people. He choreographed show-stopping satanic extravaganzas, using topless dancers from seedy San Francisco bars to grab people's attention. One of them was Susan Atkins. She played a blood-sucking vampire in LaVey's 'Witches' Sabbath', a satanic review performed at Gigi's nightclub in North Beach. She went on to become a leading member of Charles Manson's 'Family' – more on that in the Chapter 13.

This self-styled Black Pope revelled in his celebrity and boasted musician Sammy Davis Jr and veteran actor Keenan Wynn among his followers. Another high-profile member of LaVey's congregation was the actress Jayne Mansfield, who was awarded the title of the 'High Priestess of San Francisco's Church of Satan'. Mansfield's lawyer, Samuel S. Brody, was very much against her involvement with the church, however, fearing that it would hurt her public image. On 29 July 1970 Mansfield and Brody were driving in San Francisco when a truck crashed into their car, killing them both. LaVey claimed to have had prior knowledge of this disaster. He said that he had put a curse on Brody and warned Mansfield not to ride in a car with him. This was dismissed as tacky opportunism, but nonetheless it helped put LaVey and the First Church of Satan in the public eye.

LaVey was employed as an adviser on the film *Rosemary's Baby* and had a walk-on part as the devil himself. He was also technical director of the movie *The Devil's Rain*, which starred John Travolta. LaVey's show-biz involvement alienated some of his more committed followers and, when he started selling posts in the higher echelons of the church to his Hollywood friends, his followers split into other groups.

US Army officer Michael Aquino led one breakaway group and founded the rival Temple of Set, which was also recognized as a legitimate church by the Internal Revenue Service. The Temple of Set claimed that it aimed to teach 'responsible and ethical knowledge of the Black Arts' and to become 'the pre-eminent repository of the wisdom of the "left-hand path"'.

Aquino claimed to be a follower not of Satan, but of the ancient Egyptian god Set. He rushed into print *The Book of the Coming Forth by Night*, which, like LaVey's books, propounded the Crowleyan view that Satan was within man and must be released.

Despite the more secretive and intellectual approach of his satanic church, Aquino also courted theatricality. While it is easy to dismiss him as a harmless crank, Aquino had top security clearance from the US Army, served on the World Affairs Council and worked at NATO. This became alarming when it was rumoured that he had recruited at least twelve members of army intelligence into the Temple of Set. A police report noted that Aquino had worked in the army's psychological warfare department and, when the army tried to dismiss him because of his involvement with Satanism, he sued it for discrimination, arguing that his right to freedom of religion was guaranteed by the First Amendment to the Constitution. He won. Later he was promoted to lieutenant colonel, even though his increasingly fascist leanings were disturbing members of his own satanic organization.

In May 1970 eighteen-year-old Patricia Hall – also known as Inca Angelique – was arrested along with three male drifters for the rape and cat-o'-nine-tails flogging of a teenage girl in a wax museum's hall of mirrors on Bourbon Street in New Orleans. She claimed to have been baptized by LaVey and threatened to turn the arresting officers into frogs. LaVey denied all knowledge of her. She was later extradited to Florida, where she was later convicted of stabbing a sixty-six-year-old man.

Throughout the 1970s and 1980s there was a series of murders committed by confused young men, usually under the influence of drugs, who claimed Satanism as their inspiration. Many of them said their interest in the occult had begun by reading LaVey's *The Satanic Bible*.

THE HISTORY OF SATAN

The Christian idea of the devil began in Jewish tradition as a metaphor for the *yetzer hara*, or 'evil inclination', or as an agent subservient to God. Satan himself appears in the Bible, in the Book of Job. However, the popular image of Satan – the goat-like figure with horns and a tail – seems to be closely associated with the Mexican god of hell, Mictlantecuhtli. The ancient Egyptian rulers Apepi and Tiawath were depicted in similar ways, as was the Babylonian Great Duke of Hell, Astaroth, and the Persian king of demons, Asmodeus. The Greek god Dionysus was horned, half-man and half-goat, and, in Teutonic myth, there is Loki, the god of fire, who is the personification of evil.

This horned-goat image appears again in the persecution of the Knights Templar and the Cathars. Worship of the goat-creature had even made an appearance in a trial in Toulouse in 1335, during which sixty-three men and women were tried for witchcraft and sorcery, and it was said that hallucinogenic herbs mixed with alcohol were taken and the priestess would lie naked across the altar; a male worshipper would then take over the action, playing the part of the devil.

Invocations of the devil occur throughout history, and in some of the most unexpected places. In 1633, the French priest Urbain Grandier was accused of coercing nuns to perform acts of devil-worship. His home was searched and a pact he had signed with the devil was found. It was written backwards in Latin and signed in Grandier's own blood.

Around the same time, there was an outbreak of Satanism at the Monastère de Saint-Louise de Louvier in Paris. Father David, the confessor there, encouraged the nuns to go about their devotions in the nude. His successor, Father Mathurin Picard, introduced the Black Mass and got the sisters to have sexual intercourse with a devil figure reading from 'a book of blasphemies'.

Another satanic cult was discovered in Paris in 1673, which included a number of prominent members from Louis XIV's court. One of them was the Marquise de Montespan, who had been the king's mistress for twelve years. Fearing that she was losing the King's favour to a younger lover, she attended three of the 'love masses' to try and win back his ardour by acting as the nude altar table. She did briefly return to his favour!

The Hell-Fire Club was established in Britain in the eighteenth century. Members included Frederick, the Prince of Wales, and the Earl of Bute, who went on to become prime minister. Within the group, Sir Francis Dashwood conducted orgies and Black Masses and later rose to become Chancellor of the Exchequer.

8

THEOSOPHY

Uniting Science and Religion

n 1859 Charles Darwin published *The Origin of the Species* and drove a wedge between science and religion. The Theosophical Society, founded in New York in 1957, sought to breach that rift. The word 'theosophy' combined the Greek words 'theos' – God – and 'sophia'– knowledge, and the discipline aimed to meld ancient religions with science in order to liberate the psychic powers in man. It opposed the materialism of Darwinism and claimed humankind would evolve towards a more spiritual existence, while individuals would achieve a higher state though reincarnation. Masters already held the secret knowledge, but they held themselves back from merging into the 'universal oneness' to show others the way.

The driving force behind the Theosophical Society was Helena Petrovna Blavatsky, known to the world as Madame Blavatsky. She lived an extremely colourful life and, like many in her circle she claimed to possess the universal 'truth', but she seemed incapable of telling the truth in an everyday sense.

It seems she was born in the Ukraine in 1831. Her father was an army officer; her mother a novelist. From an early age, Helena claimed she could make furniture move and objects fly about, touching them only with her invisible 'astral arms'.

At seventeen she was married off to forty-year-old Nikifor

Blavatsky, a Czarist general. She claimed that the marriage was never consummated and, after three months, made her way to Constantinople. They never divorced and she retained his name for the rest of her life.

From Turkey she set off on her travels, though it is not clear where she went. She referred to this period, from 1848 to 1858, as her 'veiled time'. On various occasions she claimed to have visited the Orient, most of Asia, India, Africa, Europe, the United States and Canada, and Central and South America. During these trips, she whirled with the dervishes, learned magic with Japan's mountain-worshipping Yamabushi sect, traversed the Rockies in a covered wagon, learned the mysteries of the Mayan ruins on the Yucatán, was initiated into voodoo, became a Druze, slept in the Great Pyramid of Cheops and became an independently wealthy woman by trading in Sudanese ostrich feathers. Or so she said.

She also allegedly found the time to spend seven years in Tibet, living in a remote valley in the Himalayas with a bunch of mahatmas or masters, who revealed to her the secrets that become the basis of theosophy. Tibet, however, was closed to foreigners from 1792 until 1904 and there is absolutely no evidence she went there.

She certainly went to Egypt, though, where she took a course in snake charming and consulted a Coptic magician whom she later dismissed as a charlatan. After that she travelled around Europe with a Hungarian opera singer who claimed to have married her. There were several other putative husbands, though she claimed to her dying day that she was a virgin. For a time, a child lived with her, a hunchback who died in late childhood. He was adopted, she claimed.

In Tiflis, she briefly managed a factory producing artificial flowers. But the main thrust of her career was in spiritualism, which she practised in Russia. In England, she became an assistant to the celebrated medium Daniel Dunglas Home.

Back in Cairo in 1871, she formed the Société Spirite. Its occult teachings, she said, came from an Egyptian order called the Brotherhood of Luxor, which was so ancient and exclusive that no one had heard of it. The Société was a failure, so she made her living as a medium until she was exposed as a fraud and fled back to Europe.

In Paris in 1873, she said she had received a message from the spirit world telling her to go to the United States. At a séance in Vermont, she met newspaperman Henry Steel Olcott, who was covering the event. They hit it off immediately. Back in New York, Olcott received a letter written in gold ink on green paper, which said: 'Sister Helena will lead thee to the Golden Gate of truth'. It was signed by the Grand Master of the Brotherhood of Luxor.

Within a year, Olcott and Blavatsky were living together in an apartment in Manhattan, where she ran a salon for those interested in the occult and the esoteric arts. He was impressed by her ability to conjure things out of thin air (although the lights had to be dimmed) and by the way she summoned him by ringing an invisible bell. Olcott suggested that they form an organization to investigate all things mystical: the 'Theosophical Society'.

They seem to have picked their moment well. For two centuries, rationalism seemed to have been on the advance, and now Darwin had dealt God the creator a seemingly fatal blow. But scientific materialism offered nothing beyond the grave and it was that vacuum that the Theosophical Society aimed to fill.

Next, Madame Blavatsky dashed off the occult masterpiece *Isis Unveiled*. The Egyptian goddess, Isis, had appeared to her several times, she said, but most of the book was about the masters she claimed to have met in Tibet. They had written the book and projected it into her room in New York using 'astral light'. Despite accusations of plagiarism, the massive two-volume 1,300-page tome was an instant bestseller. It maintained that all human religions and philosophies sprang from a single hidden source – 'universal science' – and the masters had chosen her to convey it to humankind.

The success of *Isis Unveiled* gave the Theosophical Society a great fillip. Thomas Edison joined. Lodges were opened in London and Bombay. Olcott and Blavatsky then set off for India, where they added reincarnation to the mix.

Although he dressed like a Hindu and was bearded like a Sikh, Olcott became a Buddhist. He travelled widely, setting up numerous new lodges and recruiting thousands. But he had lost interest in the mystical side of theosophy and concentrated more on social reform and universal brotherhood.

Madame Blavatsky, in the meantime, plunged deeper into the occult. She wooed Alfred Percy Sinnett, editor of the British daily newspaper in India, the *Pioneer*, who was impressed when letters from the masters fell from the skies when he visited the head-quarters of the Theosophical Society. In 1881 Sinnett wrote *The Mahatma Letters*, a book extolling theosophy.

Sinnett, Blavatsky and Olcott then headed for London, leaving Blavatsky's handyman and housekeeper, Alexis and Emma Cou-lomb, in charge of the Theosophical Society's headquarters in Adyar, near Madras. The Coulombs then spilt the beans to the *Christian College Magazine*: the astral projections of the masters were nothing but turbaned dummies paraded on moonlit nights. And the letters from the masters that fell from the sky were pushed down through a crack in the ceiling.

In England the recently founded Society for Psychic Research was eager to prove Madame Blavatsky's outlandish claims for the-osophy. She agreed to co-operate with them. But in the event, the society sent an investigator out to India, who reported numerous other examples of Blavatsky's fakery. This distressed one Indian devotee so much that he set out to Tibet to see for himself, but he never made it there: he froze to death in the Himalayas.

Undeterred, Blavatsky wrote the 1,500-page *The Secret Doctrine*, in which she outlined the tenets of theosophy. Published in

1888, it purports to have been based on the world's first book, *The Stanzas of Dzyan* (which scholars down the ages have completely failed to unearth).

Even though she had been exposed as a fraud, *The Secret Doctrine* brought Madame Blavatsky new plaudits. New members flocked to the Theosophical Society and Madame Blavatsky formed a new inner circle called the Esoteric Section as a rival to the recently established Hermetic Order of the Golden Dawn. She set up the magazine *Lucifer* and published two more books, *The Key to Theosophy* and *The Voice of Silence*, before she died in 1891. Even sceptical newspapers conceded in their obituaries that she was one of the most remarkable women of the century.

ANNIE BESANT

In her will, Madame Blavatsky left instructions that Annie Wood Besant should take over as head of the Theosophical Society. As a teenager, Annie had married an elderly clergyman, but left him to become a socialist, a freethinker and an atheist. When *The Secret Doctrine* came out, Annie reviewed it favourably. Madame Blavatsky quickly recruited her and made her head of the Esoteric Section and chose Anne as her successor.

But William Q. Judge, a founding member of the Theosophical Society in New York, arrived in England and claimed to have received letters from the mahatmas telling him that he should be head of the movement. Besant said that Judge had got hold of the crayons and rice paper that Blavatsky had used and forged her handwriting to create those letters. Judge then sailed back to the US and formed the eighty-five individual chapters already established there into the Theosophical Society of America. Besant struck back with a speaking tour of America and managed to form thirty-seven new lodges there, loyal to her.

Then Besant headed to Adyar, in India. She became an advocate of Indian independence and founded the Home Rule League. Although critical of theosophy, Gandhi later acknowledged that it was Besant who brought the idea of independence to every home in the subcontinent. She adopted the fourteen-year-old Krishnamurti, said to be the long-awaited fifth Buddha – although he denied that claim in 1929.

Rudolf Steiner, head of the German chapter of the society, quit theosophy to start anthroposophy. He introduced the spiritual theory of organic farming and developed educational theories that emphasized awakening the talents that lay within each child.

9

THE MOONIES

Korea's Unification Church

The followers of Sun Myung Moon's Unification Church – more commonly known as the Moonies after its founder – are best known for their mass weddings. In 1992 Moon earned a place in the *Guinness Book of Records* after marrying 20,825 couples simultaneously in the Olympic Stadium in Seoul. Another 9,800 couples around the world joined in the ceremony by satellite link. These mass weddings are a regular feature of the cult. And it isn't just the size of these weddings that is unusual: often the couples have never met and do not even speak the same language. The marriage partners are selected by Moon more or less on a whim. The only criterion is that each person in the couple must have been a member of the sect for seven years, during which time they are supposed to have been celibate.

Sun Myung Moon was born Mun Yong Myeong in 1920 in Chongju-gun, in what is now North Korea. He later changed his name from Yong, which means dragon, to Sun and added the surname Moon. His name now literally meant Sun Shining Moon.

At the age of ten, Moon's family converted from Confucianism to Christianity, and he was brought up a Presbyterian. On Easter Sunday in 1936 he claims to have met Christ on a Korean mountainside. It was then that Moon says he received the first in a series of divine revelations that spelled out his special mission on earth. Christ apparently told Moon that he must carry out his unfinished task on earth: to bring salvation to all men and women. This prompted Moon to write his own version of the Bible entitled *Divine Principle*.

In 1945, after completing his degree in electrical engineering at Waseda University in Japan, he returned to Korea to marry his first wife, Sun Kil Choi. Shortly afterwards, however, he left his pregnant wife in Seoul while he went north to preach. In 1948 he was arrested and imprisoned by the Communists for inciting social disorder. Later his critics claimed that this involved ritual sex, while his followers said that he was imprisoned for his religious beliefs. He was released in 1950 when United Nations troops pushed the North Korean Communists back to the Chinese border during the Korean War. He was said to have walked 320 miles to Pusan, on the southern tip of the Korean Peninsula. There, as the account goes, he built a church with United States Army ration boxes and lived in a mountainside shack.

He founded the Unification Church in 1957. God, he claimed, was abandoning old-fashioned Christianity and all the Christians in the world would be absorbed into Moon's new movement. They must develop a unified front to defeat Communism. Moon sometimes claimed to be God incarnate, coming to 'conquer and subjugate the world'. At other times, he claimed to be a pure man and said that sex with him would purify the body and soul in a process known as 'blood cleansing'. The marriages of other members of the cult were considered invalid until the women had slept with Moon. As the cult grew, that proved to be an impractical measure. Moon's way around this was to insist that he arrange his disciples' weddings and, after the marriage, newly-weds were to abstain from sex for forty days while the wives slept with Moon on an 'unconscious' level.

According to the *Divine Principle*, Eve was seduced by Satan and passed on this impurity to Adam and her children. To Moon's mind, Christ's mission was to marry an ideal woman who would become perfect by sleeping with him, but he was crucified before he could fulfil his goal to create the 'perfect family'. It was now up to Moon to take over where he said Christ had left off and create the perfect God-centred family. From this would spring a God-centred nation and a God-centred world.

In 1960, after divorcing his first wife, Moon married thirty-three-year-old Hak Jan Han, who bore him twelve children. She became known as the Heavenly Mother, a counterpart to Moon's Heavenly Father. Moonies prayed in front of picture of the couple and addressed them as their 'true parents'. Followers were expected to cut ties with their real families and to sleep in communal dormitories until they married. Moonies were banned from consuming tobacco and alcohol, and had to live austere lives with long working hours and only simple food.

As far as Moon was concerned, money was the route to global dominance. The more money followers brought into the cult – through work, donations or selling flowers and trinkets on street corners – the more God-centred they were considered to be. Moon had close ties to the South Korean dictator Park Chung Hee, whose military coup in 1961 had brought Hee to power. Their friendship helped Moon to win lucrative national defence contracts for weapons produced in part in Moonie factories. Other Moonie factories produced machinery, air rifles, stone handicrafts and ginseng tea. Moon's business interests were guided by a series of companies, but Moon was chairman of each of them and exercised complete control over their operations. In 1975, the export of ginseng tea alone generated $10 million of income for Sun Myung Moon.

The Unification Church spread to from Korea to Japan, then to America, Britain and the rest of Europe. In the 1980s the Moonies moved into mainland China and in 1990 Mikhail Gorbachev allowed Moon to recruit new members in Russia. At their peak, they claimed between two and three million members worldwide.

In 1972 Moon decided to move the base of his operations to

the USA. He moved into a multi-million-dollar estate in West-chester County, where he moored two yachts for his family's use. He invested $20 million in real estate in California and New York, spending $5 million dollars on buying the New Yorker Hotel, which he turned into a hostel for his followers. During the Watergate scandal Moon held prayer meetings for President Nixon and founded the *Washington Times* newspaper to act as a rival to the *Washington Post*, the newspaper credited with bringing Nixon down. Since the Unification Church *was* recognized as a church, the Moonies enjoyed tax-free status in the US – which was fortunate, as Moon's Japanese members alone contributed some $746 million to the cult between 1975 and 1985.

Things took a turn for the worse in the 1980s when the oper-ation of a number of Moon's leading companies – such as the Collegiate Association for Research Principles and the Confedera-tion of Associations for the Unity of Societies in America – became cause for concern. In 1981 Moon brought an unsuccessful libel suit again the *Daily Mail*, which cost him £750,000, and in 1984 he was fined $250,000 and sentenced to eighteen months in prison for tax evasion. The Unification Church subsequently spent $5 million on public relations in an effort to restore Moon's good name.

Curiously, despite his long stay in America and his worldwide following, Moon never learned English. He addressed his fol-lowers in Korean and his words of wisdom were translated by Colonel Bo Hi Pak, the one-time Assistant Military Attaché at the South Korean Embassy in Washington. Nevertheless, Moon remained active in American politics. In 1994 he founded the Family Federation for World Peace and Unification, which spon-sored the Million Family March in Washington DC in 2000.

In 2003 Korean Family Federation for World Peace and Unifi-cation members started a political party in South Korea. The Party for God, Peace, Unification, and Home aimed to unite the two Korean nations on the peninsula. Despite its lack of success, and the failure of similar movements in the US, Japan and the Middle

East, Moon awarded himself the 'Crown of Peace' in Washington DC at a ceremony attended by a number of American politicians. Moon died in South Korea in 2013, aged ninety-two.

THE MARRIAGE CEREMONY

The ceremony fell into five parts:

1. The Chastening – the couple strike each other three times to signify an end to sin and preparation for a new beginning.
2. The Holy Wine – the couple share a cup of holy wine (in other words, grape juice) to symbolize their entry to God's sinless lineage.
3. The Holy Blessing – the couple exchange vows and a prayer is offered by the officiators. The couple is sprinkled with holy water.
4. The Separation Period – the couple refrains from having sexual relations for a period, usually forty days, but in some cases much longer, before consummating the marriage.
5. The Three-Day Ceremony – the official start of the couple's married life is marked by a highly symbolic ceremony over three days. This is considered to reverse the fall of Adam and Eve.

The Four Vows:

1. To become a true man or woman who practises sexual purity and lives for the sake of others.
2. To become a true husband or wife who respects their true parents' example and to establish an eternal family, which brings joy to God.
3. To become a parent who educates his or her children to follow the tradition of true love for the sake of the family and the world.
4. To create an ideal family, which contribute to world peace.

10

THE HERMETIC ORDER
OF THE GOLDEN DAWN

The Cult of Celebrity

The zenith of late-Victorian mysticism was reached in the foundation of the Hermetic Order of the Golden Dawn. Although its membership never exceeded 300 members – compared with the Theosophical Society's peak of 45,000 – it was extraordinarily influential and is considered by many to be the origin of modern occultism. While the Theosophical Society was basically a debating group within which mystical ideas were discussed, the Order of the Golden Dawn was a full-blown occult society with mysterious rituals and magical rites. Members included the Irish poet W. B. Yeats, the Satanist Aleister Crowley, the author of *Dracula*, Bram Stoker, and other contemporary celebrities who believed that they could attain occult powers.

In 1887 a bunch of ancient manuscripts came into the possession of a London-based coroner named Dr William Wynn Westcott, who was a Theosophist, a Rosicrucian and a Freemason. While leafing through the papers, Westcott came across a letter in German that instructed him to contact the Sapiens Dominator Astris – 'the wise one who lives in the stars' – who could be reached via one Fräulein Anna Sprengel. Sprengel's address was also in the letter, and so, with her help, Westcott deciphered the manuscript.

The manuscript outlined the five rituals that would produce occult power, and this discovery provided the basis of his newly established Order of the Golden Dawn. Westcott recruited a young Scotsman named Samuel Liddell Mathers to organize the rituals for him. Mathers and his wife, Moina, who was known in the cult as Vestigia, forswore sex and strove to keep themselves 'perfectly clean' for the purpose.

Under Mathers' leadership, the Golden Dawn flourished. He devised splendid costumes and elaborate rituals from the ancient texts he studied in the British Museum, and he staged the order's ceremonies with theatrical flair. W. B. Yeats was charmed by Mathers and left the Theosophical Society to join the Golden Dawn, hoping it would help him communicate with spiritual powers.

While Yeats was agitating for Irish Home Rule, Mathers dreamed of restoring a Stuart king to the throne of an independent Scotland. Mathers added MacGregor to his name, and became the self-styled Samuel Liddell MacGregor Mathers – or sometimes Count MacGregor de Glenstrae. He claimed he was the 'original Highlander', an immortal who had at one time had been King James IV of Scotland.

Things were going well for the order. Five temples were built, stretching from Edinburgh to Paris, and its membership was ever increasing. New recruits included Annie Horniman, the daughter of the wealthy tea importer, Frederick John Horniman, who later became Mathers' benefactor. Other members included the director of the Edinburgh Observatory, William Peck, the Kabbalah scholar and designer of the modern Tarot pack, A. E. Waite, writer of occult fiction, Algernon Blackwood, and psychoanalyst and novelist Dion Fortune.

The actress Florence Farr became the principal of ritual at the Isis-Urania Temple of the Golden Dawn in London. She claimed to have raised a spirit named Taphthartharath by boiling a pickled snake in a broth of magical ingredients, which included coriander seeds and gum ammoniac. The Temple's records do not record what the spirit looked like, or whether he actually appeared in physical form. However, he was said to have promised to reveal 'all the mysteries of the hidden arts and sciences'.

Despite the high profiles of these members, only Mathers and his wife had access to the secret chiefs, the Golden Dawn's equivalent to the masters of the Rosicrucians. Rendezvous were made astrally. Meeting them was like being close to a lightning bolt, Mathers claimed. A lesser man could not have survived the encounter. They also dictated the instructions for the order's rituals via clairvoyance, disembodied voices which spoke to him or Vestigia. Mathers also plundered the works of John Dee (who had been occult advisor to Elizabeth I), *The Clavicula of Solomon the King* (a medieval primer on alchemy found in the British Museum) and *The Sacred Magic of Abra-Melin the Mage* (an occult work which Mathers claimed to have discovered and translated himself).

In 1892 Mathers and Vestigia moved to Paris where, under the guidance of the secret chiefs, they lived it up at Annie Horniman's expense. Mathers also founded an inner circle called the Ordo Rosae Rubeae et Aurea Crucis – the Order of the Ruby Rose and the Cross of Gold. To join, members of the Golden Dawn had to pass all sorts of exams, with each exam pass elevating members to the next 'grade'. Funnily enough, only Mathers and Wescott reached the top grade.

Initiation rites for this new order took place in a seven-sided vault, whose walls were covered with Kabbalistic and occult symbols. Mathers or Westcott would lie in what they claimed was the coffin of the legendary founder of the Rosicrucian Order, Christian Rosenkreutz, while initiates swore on pain of death not to abuse the great power with which they were being entrusted. However, the authorities were not amused by the idea of a coroner lying around in a coffin and they forced Westcott to leave the Golden Dawn.

Annie Horniman tried to put the order's magic to good use. She and Mathers attempted to cure an epileptic child named Charlie Sewell by giving him treatment on the 'astral plane'. The poor child went through a number of rituals involving golden hexagrams and red crosses. His home was apparently exorcised of black imps and he was laden down with talismans. It is not recorded whether the boy got better.

Aleister Crowley – whom you might remember from Chapter 5 – tried to cure the mother of another member using a talisman. But the acolyte did not follow Crowley's instructions properly and nearly killed the old woman. When it was done properly, however, according to *Equinox*, an occult journal published by Crowley, the woman was apparently cured and lived until she was ninety-two.

THE END OF THE ORDER

It all ended in tears. Aleister Crowley accused the Noble Laureate W. B. Yeats of attacking him with black magic because Crowley was a better poet. Dion Fortune claimed she was plagued by demons conjured up by Vestigia Mathers. Her home was besieged by black cats and an enormous tabby cat – 'twice the size of a tiger' – also appeared indoors, though it disappeared when she stared at it. A titanic battle was being fought on the astral plane.

Vestigia had initiated a thirty-three-year-old mentally unstable woman named Norah Farnario into the Order of the Alpha and Omega, which was another offshoot of the Golden Dawn. Farnario rented a room in a croft on the Scottish island of Iona, where she told anyone who would listen to her that she was in touch with 'the world beyond'. However, without warning, she packed her bags and tried to leave the island, but it was a Sunday and the ferry did not operate on the Sabbath. The next morning, her landlady found that Farnario's bed had not been slept in. That afternoon, a search was begun.

Farnario's spread-eagled body was found high up on the moor, naked except for a silver chain around her neck and the black cloak worn by the Order of Alpha and Omega. The soles of her feet were cut and bloody as if she had been running away from something. Her face was contorted into an expression of sheer terror. In her hand was the long-bladed knife used in the order's rituals, and it seemed that she had been cutting a cross in the turf when she died. Dion Fortune claimed that Farnario had been murdered on the astral plane by Vestigia Mathers, so she left the sect to found the Fraternity of the Inner Light.

Annie Horniman also fell out with the Mathers and stopped funding their extravagant lifestyle in Paris. Mathers expelled her from the Order and backed Crowley instead, even though he was disruptive and displayed uncontrolled behaviour. The London temple refused to initiate Crowley into the Order of the Ruby Rose and the Cross of Gold, so Mathers fired its principal of ritual, Florence Farr, and replaced her with Crowley.

When Crowley turned up at the Golden Dawn's headquarters, Farr called the police and had him removed. He then returned in full Highland garb, wearing the black mask of Osiris and brandishing a dagger. Again, he was refused entry, so he visited Mathers in Paris, who was shaking some dried peas in a sieve and calling on the demons Typhon-Set and Beelzebub to strike down his enemies, including Farr. This failed and Mathers was expelled from the Golden Dawn.

Yeats then took over the order, but he could not hold the Golden Dawn together. The poet finally gave up and the order ceased in 1923.

11

SCIENTOLOGY

Faith in Science Fiction

The Church of Scientology was estimated at one time to have between 100,000 and 200,000 members worldwide. While the numbers seem to have declined significantly in recent years, it remains one of the wealthiest, most secretive and most litigious cults of our time. It was started by science-fiction writer L. Ron Hubbard in 1952, whom, as you may remember from Chapter 5, was the 'scribe' for Jack Parsons' experiments with sexual magick before he ran off with Parsons' former girlfriend and his money. Scientology initially began as a form of psychotherapy, but was incorporated as the Church of Scientology in New Jersey in 1953. The Church of Scientology of California, which became the cult's headquarters, was founded in Los Angeles in 1954. Its principal overseas operation was started in 1959 at Saint Hill Manor, near East Grinstead in Sussex, England.

Lafayette Ronald Hubbard was born in 1911 in Tilden, Nebraska. A promising student at school, Hubbard went to George Washington University, where he studied physics, but he left after a year and began to write pulp science-fiction stories for magazines.

He joined the Navy during the Second World War. Scientologists claim that he was a war hero, but his service record states that he was struck down by a duodenal ulcer and never saw action. The

Church of Scientology claims that authorities falsified the record because Hubbard had been involved in top-secret operations.

In his novel *The Voyage of the Space Beagle*, Hubbard's friend and fellow science-fiction writer A. E. van Vogt created the fictional 'Science of Nexialism', an advanced and benevolent form of psychological conditioning. Hubbard took this idea seriously and came up with his own version, publishing an article on 'Dianetics' in the magazine *Astounding Science Fiction* in May 1950. It was so well received that Hubbard quickly wrote the follow-up book, *Dianetics: The Modern Science of Mental Health*, which became a bestseller.

According to Hubbard, the unconscious or 'reactive' mind stores the trauma of every unpleasant thing that has ever happened. The aim of Dianetics was to rid the individual of these unconscious memories or engrams and aid them to achieve a state which they called 'Clear'. The process of becoming 'Clear' was enacted via a technique called 'auditing', which takes the individual back to the source of the engram.

Dianetics groups sprang up all over America. Hubbard himself set up the Hubbard Dianetic Research Foundation, but in 1952 it went bankrupt and Hubbard sold off his share in it, which included his copyright to *Dianetics: The Modern Science of Mental Health*, to Don Purcell. Hubbard then set up the Association of Scientologists and sued Purcell for the use of his ideas, eventually winning back the copyright.

Scientology became a church, largely for tax purposes, but its adherents insist upon its status as a form of psychology rather than a religion. The next development in Scientology was the introduction of the E-meter. It functioned a bit like a primitive lie detector, but it was supposed to measure engrams rather than falsehoods. In 1963 America's Food and Drug Administration raided the Church of Scientology in Washington and seized all the E-meters on the grounds that it was illegal in the US to practise any form of medical diagnosis or therapy unless medically qualified. A 1969 court ruling allowed Scientologists to sell E-meters only if they were labelled as 'ineffective'.

But simply flushing out the engrams and making an individual become 'Clear' was not good enough for the Church of Scientology. Instead, recruits would have further ladders to climb until they had attained the elusive last stage and crossed the 'bridge to total freedom'. The hierarchical grades of membership continued to multiply and, of course, the knowledge they promulgated had to be kept secret. However, when defectors escaped, information inevitably leaked out.

For example, the third level, known as the 'Wall of Fire', asserts that the galaxy was overpopulated seventy-five million years ago. The story goes that the dictator Xenu persuaded billions of beings from the seventy-five inhabited planets in the Galactic Federation to come to Teegeeack, or the planet we call Earth. Xenu then chained these new inhabitants up in the volcanoes on Hawaii and bombarded them with nuclear bombs. This released their inner selves, or Theta beings, from their bodies. Millions of these Thetans are said to cluster around every one of us, bringing with them their engrams, which are responsible for sexual perversion, religion and all the other troubles in the world. To 'Clear' them away, the auditor must take the initiate back seventy-five million years to remove the cause of the problem.

Governments around the world soon began having problems with the Church of Scientology, especially over its claims for tax-exempt status as a religious organization from money derived from its members. In 1965 the Australian government set up a Board of Inquiry. Its report concluded: 'Scientology is evil, its techniques evil, its practice a serious threat to the community, medically, morally and socially, and its adherents sadly deluded and often mentally ill.'

Furthermore, the report stated that Scientology 'is a delusional belief system, based on fiction and fallacies and propagated by falsehood and deception'. The Board of Inquiry dismissed the cult as 'the world's largest organization of unqualified persons engaged in the practice of dangerous techniques which masquerade as mental therapy'.

In 1968 the British government banned foreign Scientologists from coming to the UK to study or work. That ban was lifted in 1980, but in a British court case in 1984, the judge came to much the same conclusion as the Australian Board of Inquiry: 'Scientology is both immoral and socially obnoxious,' he said. 'In my judgement it is corrupt, sinister and dangerous. It is based on lies and deceit and has as its real objective money and power for Mr Hubbard, his wife and those close to him at the top.'

While Scientology may have made L. Ron Hubbard very rich, things were not going too smoothly for him in his personal life. His 'supposed' daughter, Alexis, Hubbard declared, had in fact been fathered by Jack Parsons, and in 1959, his oldest son, Ron Junior, publicly declared that his father was insane.

In 1966 Hubbard quit as head of the Church of Scientology, although he remained the power behind the throne. He spent the rest of his life sailing around the world, staying offshore for tax purposes. His three sea-going vessels were crewed by an elite band of Scientologists, the so-called Messengers, largely made up of teenage girls. They did everything for him and were subject to stringent punishment, such as being thrown overboard and locked in cupboards, for even the most minor infractions.

Hubbard declared that critics of Scientology should be investigated and undermined. Any tactic, as far as he was concerned, was fair game to employ against their opponents who might be 'tricked, sued or lied to or destroyed'. Dirty tricks, such as psychological ploys, character assassination and close surveillance, were used to blacken the name of individuals who spoke out against Scientology.

The church set up a secret intelligence unit called the 'Guardian's Office' to infiltrate organizations which were deemed threatening to Scientology. Top of the list was the Internal Revenue Service

(IRS). In a covert operation in the early 1970s, Scientology members stole hundreds of documents from the IRS offices in Los Angeles. The US government responded by sending in the FBI, which resulted in the arrest of nine senior Scientologists, including Hubbard's third wife, Mary Sue.

Hubbard was convicted of fraud in 1978 and sentenced *in absentia* to four years in prison. Shortly afterwards, Hubbard had a series of heart attacks and a young acolyte named David Miscavige began to take over. By 1982, Miscavige was in full control of the cult, though this ultimately led to a split in the organization

By that time, Hubbard was living such a reclusive life in his luxury motor-home in California that few people know for certain when he died. Some say it was as early as 1983, though his demise was not publicly announced until January 1986.

CONTINUING CONTROVERSY

There can be little doubt that the Church of Scientology funds a number of worthwhile drug rehabilitation, environmental and human rights programmes, though it still opposes mainstream psychiatry. Meanwhile, disaffected members claimed that Miscavige had departed from Hubbard's original philosophy and formed independent groups under the umbrella title the Free Zone.

In many countries there are disputes over the Church of Scientology's status as a not-for-profit organization, although its tax-exempt status was restored in the US in 1993. Movie stars such as John Travolta and Tom Cruise remain eloquent advocates, with Cruise being awarded the inaugural Scientology Freedom Medal of Valor by Miscavige in 2004.

12

THE PROCESS CHURCH
OF THE FINAL JUDGEMENT

Christ, Lucifer and Satan

The Process Church of the Final Judgement was the brainchild of Robert de Grimston Moor. He became a Scientologist while still a student, and by 1962 he had become a senior member and high-ranking officer of the Church of Scientology in the UK. However, de Grimston soon went off to form his own cult, the Process Church, which actively promoted murder. Charles Manson was a member and the church had connections with other notable murderers in the late 1960s and 1970s.

Robert de Grimston met Mary Anne MacLean at the Church of Scientology's London headquarters in Fitzrovia. At the time she was working as a nightclub hostess on the fringes of the social circle that included Christine Keeler and Mandy Rice-Davies. One of her boyfriends was the osteopath and artist Stephen Ward, who was the only man to stand trial in the Profumo scandal. Ward was fascinated by the occult.

De Grimston and MacLean set up an informal group that practised what they called compulsion therapy. This attempted to free participants of compulsive behaviour by examining the reasons behind it. By 1963 the group's ideas began to deviate from Scientology, so de Grimston, MacLean and their followers left to set up their own sect. They established the Process Church of the Final Judgement, whose members believed, like the Cathars, in both God and Lucifer.

The Process Church had a particularly broad take on the concept of free will. Jews, they said, had chosen to be exterminated in the Nazi gas chambers. People born disabled had chosen that course in a past life. These weird ultra-libertarian ideas struck a chord in the swinging London of the 1960s. Beatniks and bikers flocked to join the new religion, but the Process Church put most of its effort into recruiting the beautiful people – the wealthy and well-connected who would fund the church and introduce it to the upper reaches of society.

By March 1966 the Process Church had enough money to lease a mansion in Balfour Place, Mayfair. De Grimston, MacLean and twenty-five other cult members moved in, along with six Alsatian dogs. On a trip to Mexico, Process members began practising the sex-and-Satanism rites carried out by Aleister Crowley.

Back in London, de Grimston opened an occult bookshop, started publishing *Process* magazine and tried to recruit the new young pop glitterati – particularly the Beatles and the Rolling Stones – with some success. Marianne Faithfull, clutching a rose and pretending to be dead, posed on the front cover of the first issue.

In 1967 de Grimston published his first book, *As It Is*, in which he outlined his philosophy. Christ had said: 'Love your enemy'; Christ's enemy was Satan. So, it followed that anyone who followed Christ should love Satan too. This love would eventually break down the schism between Christ and Satan, good and evil and, on the Day of Judgement, Christ and Satan would be reconciled. De Grimston outlined how to hasten this in his second book, *Jehovah on War*, by saying simply: 'Thou shalt kill'.

De Grimston believed that a spree of motiveless killings would herald the Final Judgement, since the Battle of Armageddon preceded the Day of Judgement in the Book of Revelation. De Grimston did not think the numerous human sacrifices Crowley claimed to have made were enough. He preached that life should be one long murderous ritual.

In the summer of 1967 the cult moved to San Francisco and set up in the centre of hippie counter-culture, the Haight-Ashbury district. Their headquarters were at 407 Cole Street. Just two blocks down the street, at number 636, there lived an ex-convict and drifter named Charles Manson.

Later, the US wing of the Process Church moved to Los Angeles and Manson followed. There, Hell's Angels and drug addicts from Sunset Strip, as well as minor musicians and movie actors, became willing converts. The Process Church tried to hook up with the First Church of Satan, but Anton LaVey dismissed DeGrimston and his followers as 'kooks'.

Process Church members wore black suits and capes with the satanic Goat of Mendes embroidered in red on the back. They wore silver crucifixes, many of them inverted in the satanic manner, around their necks. Another symbol of the Process Church was four Ps joined together at the centre, making a symbol like a swastika with semi-circles at the end of its 'arms'.

The sect was divided into three factions that would reunite on the Day of Judgement. One group followed Christ and was strait-laced and puritanical. The second followed Lucifer and enjoyed sex, drugs and rock 'n' roll. The third followed Satan and believed in blood sacrifice and violence.

Process magazine gave equal space to the three opposing factions. The fourth issue was devoted to sex. In it, the Christian faction argued that sex was a defilement. The followers of Lucifer called for cult members to wash away 'all pointless guilt, all worthless fear, all futile shame ... all embarrassment and the crippling bonds of self-restraint', while the Satanists urged recruits to 'sink down in the decadence of excessive self-indulgence. Let no so-called sin, perversion or depravity escape your searching senses; partake of them all of them to overflowing ... There is no dialectic but death.'

Even though the Process Church seemed to treat the three factions even-handedly, de Grimston's personal beliefs skewed towards the satanic. The cover of the 'Sex' issue of *Process* magazine featured a naked girl spread-eagled on an altar. She is surrounded by hooded worshippers and above her is an inverted cross. Whichever faction recruits joined, they were expected to spend some time in satanic worship.

The fifth issue of *Process* magazine focused on fear. In it, de Grimston told cult members that 'by seeking out fear in living experience, we become fear itself'. No doubt these words were taken to heart by Charles Manson, who, by this time, had joined the Process Church. De Grimston referred to the cult as the 'Family'. Manson, who had just formed a 'Family' of this own, contributed an article to the sixth issue of *Process*: the 'Death' issue.

During his time in California, de Grimston published his third great work of cult philosophy, *Satan on War*. In it, he wrote: 'Release the fiend that lies dormant within you, for he is strong and ruthless and his power is far beyond the bounds of human frailty.'

Soon after, the Process Church broke up, largely because many of the original members from London had gone to the US on ninety-day tourist visas which they had long outstayed. New branches of the Process Church were set up in Boston, Chicago, Dallas, New Orleans, Toronto and Cambridge, Massachusetts. De Grimston and MacLean headed for New York and established a branch in fashionable Greenwich Village.

BLOOD SACRIFICE AND MURDER

Although the Process Church left California behind, not all its followers followed suit. A large number of dead dogs were found in the area around Santa Cruz, just south of San Francisco. Most were Alsatians. They had been beheaded, mutilated, skinned and some had even been drained of their blood. District Attorney Peter Chang described Santa Cruz as the 'murder capital of the world'.

On 13 July 1970 twenty-two-year-old Stanley Dean Baker was stopped by the California Highway Patrol. In his pocket he had a well-thumbed copy of Anton LaVey's *Satanic Bible* and a finger. 'I have a problem,' he told the police. 'I am a cannibal.'

Baker claimed to be a practising Satanist and a member of a blood-drinking cult in Wyoming, which was an offshoot of the Process Church. They sacrificed dogs during their ceremonies and drank their blood. The cult called itself the Four P Movement – or Four Pi for short.

During his trial, Baker was linked to the murder of forty-year-old Robert Salem. When Salem's murdered body was found in his San Francisco apartment, there was a piece of paper with a crude drawing of a crucified man and the word 'Zodiac' on it. On Salem's stomach was carved the circle and crosshairs akin to those of a gunsight that became the symbol of the Zodiac Killer, an as yet unidentified serial killer who was responsible for as many as forty murders in the Bay Area of San Francisco in the 1970s. In jail, Dean Baker applied to join the First Church of Satan, but was refused admission.

There is evidence that David Berkowitz, convicted of the 'Son of Sam' murders in New York in 1978, was a member of the 'Twenty-Two Disciples of Hell', which had links to both the Process Church and the Order of Oriental Templars.

13

THE MANSON FAMILY

Helter Skelter

C harles Manson's 'Family' was a murderous, quasi-hippie commune based in California. Manson's despicable ideas seem to have derived from his time in the Process Church, while his chief lieutenant and hitwoman, Susan Atkins, was a Satanist with connections to Anton LaVey and his First Church of Satan from Chapter 7. In 1969 the Family terrorized Los Angeles with a series of nine murders which were committed in order to provoke a race war. Their homicidal campaign was called 'Helter Skelter', inspired by the track of the same title from the Beatles' *White Album*. It appears Manson was unaware that a helter skelter was the name for a spiral slide found at funfairs; he assumed it had something to do with hell.

Charles Manson was born 'No Name Maddox' in Cincinnati, Ohio, the illegitimate son of a teenage prostitute named Kathleen Maddox and a drugstore cowboy who went by the name of Colonel Scott. Kathleen's brief marriage to William Manson was the source of Charles's surname.

After his mother was jailed for robbing a petrol station, Manson was sent to live with relatives. Kathleen and her son were briefly reunited on her release, but then she met a man who wanted her but not her child. Manson was sent to an orphanage but was soon kicked out for his surly manner and constant thieving.

In his teens Manson became a drifter and was arrested for stealing food. He was sent to Indiana Boys' School, from which he escaped eighteen times. In 1951 he was arrested again for theft and served four years in a federal reformatory.

Jailed again in 1958, Manson ended up in the federal penitentiary on McNeil Island in Washington State, where he alleged he had been repeatedly raped. He claimed that many of his assailants were black, which reinforced his racist world-view.

After his release in 1967, the thirty-two-year-old Manson became introduced to a new generation that was turning on, tuning in and dropping out. He headed for the Haight-Ashbury district of San Francisco, the centre of this counter-culture, where he had his first experience with LSD.

To earn a living, he bought a guitar and began busking. He got involved with the Process Church from Chapter 12 and he soon became a sought-after guru.

His first female follower was Mary Brunner, a naive and impressionable librarian. Soon he picked up another girl called Linda 'Darlene' Kasabian, who left her husband and two children and stole $5,000 from a friend to join the fledgling Family. Manson quickly discovered that he could control his female followers through sex.

When the Process Church moved down to Los Angeles, Mary bought a VW camper-van and they headed south down the coast. Once there, Manson intended to establish himself as a rock star.

In Venice Beach he met Lynette 'Squeaky' Fromme, an emotionally vulnerable woman with family problems. Manson brought her back to Mary Brunner and Kasabian, and the four of them became the nucleus of the Family. Soon Manson's cult comprised a harem of young women and a number of docile men, controlled, like his female followers, with doses of LSD.

Other early recruits included Patricia Krenwinkel, a legal clerk who abandoned everything to be with Manson, and Leslie Van Houten, a nineteen-year-old drop out.

Susan Atkins was Manson's next recruit. You might remember her from Chapter 7 as the topless dancer and bar-room hustler who became involved in Anton LaVey's First Church of Satan. She became Manson's closest aide and used acid-fuelled orgies to plant Satanist ideas in his followers' receptive minds. She managed to convince Manson that his own name was significant. He was Man-son, the Son of Man or Christ, and, according to her twisted logic, he was also the devil.

One of the few men in the commune was twenty-three-year-old former high-school football star from Farmersville, Texas, Charles 'Tex' Watson. He had once been an honours student, but in Manson's hands he became a mindless automaton. Bruce Davis and Steve Grogan joined them, as did Bobby Beausoleil, a protégé of underground film-maker Kenneth Anger, who himself was a follower of Aleister Crowley – the self-styled 'wickedest man in the world' from Chapter 5 – and a member of LaVey's magic circle.

Dennis Wilson, of the 1960s Californian band the Beach Boys, was particularly fascinated by Manson and his lifestyle. The Family free-loaded on Wilson and used him in order to hang around the fringes of the Hollywood scene.

When the Beatles' *White Album* came out, Manson believed that the songs in it contained a message directed at him and the Family. 'Sexy Sadie' was Susan Atkins, whose real name *was* Sadie. 'Piggies' were those who sneered at the police and the establishment. 'Blackbird' was a call for black people to revolt. 'Revolution 9' referred to Chapter Nine of the Book of Revelation, the coming of the Apocalypse and the Exterminating Angel. And for Manson, the track 'Helter Skelter' heralded what he saw as the inevitable race war.

Manson started writing his own songs and took one of his compositions to the successful West Coast musician Gary Hinman. After learning that Hinman had recently inherited $20,000, he sent Mary Brunner, Susan Atkins and Bobby Beausoleil to Hinman's house to steal the money and murder Hinman for refusing to help take Manson's song to the top of the charts.

Hinman was shot and stabbed and left to bleed to death. Atkins wrote 'Political piggies' on the wall in his blood alongside a cat's paw-print, the logo of the Black Panther Party. Hinman's body was discovered four days later, along with Beausoleil's fingerprints. Beausoleil was convicted of murder and sent to jail – and managed not to implicate Atkins or Manson.

THE TATE AND LABIANCA MURDERS

Manson's next move was to try to get his song recorded by Terry Melcher, the son of the actress Doris Day, but Melcher failed to see the potential of Manson's material. On 8 August 1969 Manson sent Tex Watson, Susan Atkins, Patricia Krenwinkel and Linda Kasabian to Melcher's remote home at 10050 Cielo Drive in the Hollywood Hills. Melcher, however, had moved out and the film director Roman Polanski was living there, but he happened to be shooting a movie in London at the time. Polanski's wife, the movie star Sharon Tate, who was eight months pregnant at the time, was at home, along with her guests Abigail Folger, Voytek Frykowski and the celebrity hairdresser Jay Sebring.

Kasabian lost her nerve and stayed outside, but Tex Watson shinned up a nearby telegraph pole and cut the phone lines. As he, Atkins and Krenwinkel entered the grounds of the property they came across eighteen-year-old Steven Parent, who had been visiting the resident caretaker. Brandishing a knife and a .22-calibre revolver, Watson ignored Parent's pleas for mercy, slashed his hand and pumped four bullets into his chest.

Once inside the house, they rounded up the occupants. While Atkins was tying them up, Jay Sebring broke free and made a lunge for the gun. Watson shot him in the armpit, then stabbed him seven times.

Voytek Frykowski attacked Watson, who beat him with the butt of his pistol. Frykowski managed to stagger to the door, screaming for help, but the women stabbed and shot at him until he died. Abigail Folger also tried to make a break for it, but Krenwinkel caught up with her halfway across the lawn and Watson stabbed her to death. Sharon Tate begged for the life of her unborn child, but Krenwinkel held Tate down while Atkins stabbed her sixteen times. The killers wrote the word 'Pig' on the front door in Tate's blood. Back at the Spahn Ranch, Manson celebrated this great victory with an orgy.

Two days later Watson, Kasabian, Krenwinkel, Atkins, Grogan and Leslie Van Houten set out again, this time accompanied by Manson. They broke into a house in the Silver Lake area that belonged to Leno LaBianca and his wife Rosemary. The couple woke to find Manson holding a gun in their faces. He tied them up and told them that they would not be harmed. Manson left with Kasabian, Atkins and Grogan, and sent Watson, Leslie Van Houten and Krenwinkel back into the house. Watson stabbed Leno LaBianca twelve times and carved the word 'War' on his abdomen. Then Watson and Krenwinkel stabbed Rosemary forty-one times. They wanted Van Houten to join in, so she reluctantly stabbed Rosemary sixteen times in the buttocks. Using their victim's blood, they wrote 'Death to pigs' and 'Rise' on the wall and 'Healter [sic] Skelter' on the refrigerator door.

The police were slow to connect the Tate and LaBianca murders to the Hinman case. Since the killings had not sparked the race war they had hoped for, the Family began to break up. Susan Atkins fled and turned to prostitution. When arrested, she admitted to being in Hinman's house when he was murdered. In jail she bragged to her cellmate about the other murders – and blamed Manson.

The Manson Trial began on 15 June 1970. It was unique. Never in the history of American jurisprudence had a defendant been charged with mass murder by proxy, as Manson had not actually killed anyone himself. He was convicted, along with Beausoleil, Atkins, Krenwinkel and Van Houten. Bruce Davis and Steve Grogan were also convicted for the murder of Spahn ranchman Donald 'Shorty' Shea, whom Manson had thought was a police spy. They were all sentenced to death but, before the sentence could be carried out, the death penalty was abolished in California and their sentences were commuted to life imprisonment.

Manson's fame continues to this day. In 2014 he planned to marry a young female visitor, fifty-three years his junior, but called it off when he discovered that the marriage was a ploy to gain possession of his body, which she planned to display in a glass case after his death. He died in jail in 2017.

14

DRUIDS

The Cult of the Celts

Julius Caesar recorded that in Britain, as in Gaul, there were Druids. What little is known of the ancient Druids comes from Caesar's writings and other Ancient Roman sources – which are likely to be inaccurate as the Romans sought to suppress the Druidic order. In his writing, Caesar particularly dwelt on the Druidic practice of human sacrifice, a ceremony in which victims were burned alive in a huge wicker effigy – although this may well have been Ancient Roman anti-Druid propaganda. There are also passing references to Druids in medieval tales, wherein they were portrayed as sorcerers who opposed the coming of Christianity. It is from these shadowy beginnings that modern Druidry has been conjured.

When the United Kingdom was established by the Act of Union between England and Scotland in 1707, the non-English inhabitants of the British Isles sought to define their separate identity within the new state. Long before, the Scottish, Irish, Welsh and Cornish – although very different people – had assumed a common Celtic heritage to draw a distinction between them and the English. Between the fifth and first centuries BC, it was said, the Celts, a Germanic tribe, had migrated westwards to the British Isles. There is no hard and fast historical evidence for this, although when the Romans arrived in Britain they commented on the existence of Celts there – but the name 'Celt' may merely have been a catch-all term for any northern-European person who was not a Roman.

In 1717 the Irish philosopher John Toland founded the Ancient Order of Druids, and in 1726 he published his (specious) *History of the Druids* to demonstrate his knowledge of Gaelic. Nevertheless, as the 'Celtic revival' of the eighteenth and nineteenth centuries gained pace, the practice of Druidism also took hold in Britain.

In 1792 Welsh stonemason Edward Williams, who liked to style himself Iolo Morganwg – 'Iolo of Glamorgan' – began to perform what he said were 'ancient' Druidic ceremonies on Primrose Hill in London. The Ancient Order of Druids still performs ceremonies there today (and on the roof of the McDonald's at Tower Hill!) on the equinoxes. Williams also established the Welsh festival of Eisteddfod in 1819, but how deeply these events are rooted in Druidic tradition it is hard to say; particularly since Williams appears to have forged many of the 'early' Welsh documents he refers to himself.

The nineteenth-century Welsh nationalist William Price fled to France after a failed uprising in 1839, and he saw what he took to be ancient Celtic relics in the Louvre. Upon his return to Britain he attempted to revive Druidism as the religion of the Celts. Styling himself an arch-druid, he became a leader in the growing Neo-Druidic movement, and walked around with an engraved staff.

In 1871 Price published a book in a language he claimed was Ancient Welsh, but which seems to have been of his own invention. Then, on his eighty-first birthday, in 1881, he married a twenty-one-year-old farm girl in a Druidic ceremony at the Rocking Stone in Pontypridd. Two years later they had a son, whom Price named Iesu Grist – Welsh for Jesus Christ – but the child died at just five months old. Price decided to cremate his body, but was attacked by an angry mob and arrested by the police for what they believed to be the illegal disposal of a corpse. In court Price successfully argued that there was no law against cremation and the case led to the Cremation Act of 1902.

Even though several Druid lodges were closed down in the wake of the French Revolution when secretive societies were viewed with suspicion, by 1831 there were 193 lodges with over 200,000 members in Britain. However, in the 'Great Secession' of 1833, around half of these members split off from the Grand Lodge (the ruling body of the Ancient Order of Druids previously) to form a new United Ancient Order of Druids. Winston Churchill was a member of the Albion Lodge of the Ancient Order of Druids in Oxford.

One of the tenuous ceremonies performed by modern-day Druids takes place at Stonehenge at the summer solstice. Stonehenge was first linked to the Celts by the diarist John Aubrey in the 1690s, but the building of Stonehenge had nothing to do with any people who might have come to the British Isles after the fifth century BC, as the monument we can still see was completed a thousand years earlier. Nevertheless, in 1908 the then Chief Druid, George Watson McGregor, campaigned for the right to worship at the stones. English Heritage now opens the site for thousands of Druids to attend to see the sun rise over the Heel Stone. At these ceremonies the Druids wear white cloaks and hoods.

Druidism now comes in numerous varieties. Fifteen different groups came together to form the Council of British Druid Orders in 1989. These now include the Ancient Order of Druids, the Order of Bards, Ovates and Druids and the British Druid Order. The Secular Order of Druids was established in 1986 to further that most ancient of Celtic philosophies ... environmentalism.

One of the most popular sects is the Druid Clan of Dana, based at Clonegal Castle in Eire. It is one of the three branches of the Fellowship of Isis, founded in 1976 by the Reverend Lawrence Durdin-Robertson, who could apparently trace the Robertson lineage back to Ancient Egypt via the Celts.

The United Ancient Order of Druids arrived in the US in the 1830s, with the first lodge established in New York City in 1839. By 1896 it had 17,000 members, rising to 35,000 in 1923. Later on that century, orders were also established in California, Melbourne, in Australia, and New Zealand.

The United Ancient Order of Druids in California was established in Placerville in 1860, although it claims to have no association with the Druids who appear at Stonehenge. It is organized into Groves, Circles and Chapters: Groves are the original men's group, Circles are the women's auxiliary groups, and the Chapter is a group for both male and female Druids to meet together.

The first lodge in Australia was established in Melbourne in 1851. The Supreme Grand Lodge of Australia and New Zealand followed in 1912, with Alderman James J. Brenan, veteran Grand Secretary of the Victorian Grand Lodge of the United Ancient Order of Druids, as its Supreme Arch Druid.

THE DRUIDS OF GAUL

Julius Caesar is our primary source on the Druids. He is said to have come across the Druids in *Gallia Comata*, or in the region known as 'long-haired Gaul' – the area to the north and west of Provence and Narbonne Gaul. This is what he had to say about them:

Throughout all Gaul there are two orders of those men who are of any rank and dignity: for the commonality is held almost in the condition of slaves, and dares to undertake nothing of itself, and is admitted to no deliberation. The greater part, when they are pressed either by debt, or the large amount of their tributes, or the oppression of the more powerful, give themselves up in vassalage to the nobles, who possess over them the same rights without exception as masters over their slaves. But of these two orders, one is that of the Druids, the other that of the knights. The former are engaged in things sacred, conduct the public and the private sacrifices, and interpret all matters of religion. To these a large number of the young men resort for the purpose of instruction, and they are in great honour among them. For they determine respecting almost all controversies, public and private; and if any crime has been perpetrated, if murder has been committed, if there be any dispute about an inheritance, if any about boundaries, these same persons decide it; they decree rewards and punishments; if any one, either in a private or public capacity, has not submitted to their decision, they interdict him from the sacrifices ... Over all these Druids one presides, who possesses supreme authority among them. Upon his death, if any individual among the rest is pre-eminent in dignity, he succeeds; but, if there are many equal, the election is made by the suffrages of the Druids; sometimes they even contend for the presidency with arms. These assemble at a fixed period of the year in a consecrated place in the territories of the Carnutes, which is reckoned the central region of the whole of Gaul. Hither all, who have disputes, assemble from every part, and submit to their decrees and determinations. This institution is supposed to have been devised in Britain, and to have been brought over from it into Gaul; and now those who desire to gain a more accurate knowledge of that system generally proceed thither for the purpose of studying it. The Druids do not go to war, nor pay tribute together with the rest; they have an exemption from military service and a dispensation in all matters. Induced by such great advantages, many embrace this profession of their own accord, and many are sent to it by their parents and relations. They are said there to learn by heart a great number of verses; accordingly some remain in the course of training for twenty years. Nor do they regard it lawful to commit these to writing, though in almost all other matters, in their public and private transactions, they use Greek characters.

15

THE PEOPLE'S TEMPLE

Massacre at Jonestown

Religious leader Jim Jones, the founder of the People's Temple, was responsible for the death of over 900 of his followers. As a precocious child with an intense fascination with religion, he would deliver hellfire-and-damnation speeches at the funerals he held for dead cats. But some saw a more sinister side to his interest in felines. A childhood acquaintance recalled: 'Some of the neighbours would have cats missing and we always thought he was using them for sacrifices.' Many years later he organized a mass suicide in a supposed Utopia he had set up in the jungles of Guyana.

James Warren Jones grew up in the small town of Lynn, Indiana, a town that depended on one thriving local industry: coffin-making. Jones's father was the local barfly, redneck and a lifelong member of the Ku Klux Klan. Jones's mother believed in spells, omens and black magic. She subscribed to the *National Geographic* and her bedtime stories for her son featured imaginary journeys up the Amazon to visit the head-hunters there. She predicted her son would one day be the champion of the poor and the weak, believing he was destined to leave his mark on the world.

He began as a door-to-door recruiter for a Methodist mission and soon became an unordained preacher, but the largely white congregation did not like the black people Jones brought in. Nor did they like his hell-and-damnation sermons, or his claim that he had once met God on the train to Philadelphia. He was thrown out from the church.

At the age of twenty-two Jones founded a small church in a rundown area of Indianapolis, which had various names until it became, in its final incarnation, the People's Temple Christian Church Full Gospel. Jones studied the ministry of African-American spiritual leader Father Divine of the International Peace Movement in Philadelphia and put on his own theatrical displays of healing. He convinced his followers to spew up chicken livers, claiming they were cancers Jones had cast out from their bodies. His success at building a truly multi-racial congregation – one of the first in America – brought his church under attack by segregationists, who threw dead cats into his church and smashed his windows.

By the early 1960s, Jones was married to Marceline Baldwin and they had adopted eight Korean and black children. He took his young family away for two years of missionary work in the *favelas* in Brazil. On their way back to the US they stopped off in British Guiana, which was to become the independent country of Guyana in 1966.

Upon his return, discovering that America was riven by race riots and protests against the war in Vietnam, Jones promised to take his followers to a 'promised land'. He relocated the People's Temple to Redwood Valley, California, where he soon began to wield considerable political power. Politicians were quick to back a man who promised to deliver the block vote of a congregation numbering several thousand. San Francisco's mayor, George Moscone, appointed Jones as chairman of the city's housing authority and, during the 1976 presidential campaign, Jones dined with Rosalynn Carter, the wife of presidential hopeful Jimmy Carter.

In affluent Redwood Valley, Jones attracted a white, middle-class congregation. One of them was an ambitious young lawyer named Tim Stoen. Jones's growing political influence secured Stoen the plum job of Assistant District Attorney in San Francisco, and the price tag for that was access to Stoen's young wife, Grace. In January 1972 Grace gave birth to a son, John-John. The birth certificate recorded the father as Tim Stoen, but in a legal affidavit Stoen stated that he requested Jones to sire a child by his wife 'in the steadfast hope that the said child will become the devoted follower of Jesus Christ and be instrumental in bringing God's kingdom here on earth, as has been his wonderful natural father'. The affidavit was witnessed by Marceline, Jones's wife.

Jones began to use his female followers as a harem. For him, sex quickly became more about power than pleasure. By seducing members of his congregation, he loosened the connection between them and their partners and bound them both closer to the Temple. All sexual contact with outsiders, however, was banned and sexual relations between other members of the congregation required the Temple's specific approval.

Jones also had sex with men, and in 1973 he was picked up for making sexual overtures to an undercover policeman in the toilet of a cinema in Los Angeles during a matinee of *Jesus Christ Superstar*. By then Jones had enough influence to get the charges dropped and the arrest record sealed. But he became paranoid, claiming that his phone was being tapped by the FBI and that he was being followed by government agents.

Sex was a frequent topic of discussion at the Temple's all-important Planning Commission. Jones would force members to publicly confess their sexual fears and fantasies, sentencing those who were less than forthcoming to long periods of celibacy. At one meeting Jones forced one white man to perform cunnilingus on a black woman.

When their sixteen-year-old daughter was spanked for having a friend Jones suspected was a traitor, former Seventh Day Adventists Elmer and Deanna Mertle decided to leave the organization. This was difficult, as they had given everything they owned to the Temple. Dismissed as traitors, they were accused of stealing incriminating documents from the church and Jones threatened to smear Elmer as a child molester. Fearing for their safety, the Mertles changed their name and kept sworn affidavits charging Jones with all manner of indecent behaviour in a safe-deposit box in case they came to harm.

That same year, 1997, Jones was named 'Humanitarian of the Year' by the *Los Angeles Herald-Examiner*, and the Foundation for Religion in America named Jones one of their '100 Outstanding Clergymen in America'. On Memorial Day, he was invited to speak at a rally in San Francisco to help campaign for an anti-suicide barrier to be built on the Golden Gate Bridge. Jones's speech began as a condemnation of suicide but turned into a blanket endorsement for it.

Jones had spoken of 'revolutionary suicide' as early as 1973. His followers, he said, were to kill themselves and he was to stay alive to explain why they had done it. On New Year's Day in 1976 he told his congregation that they had to drink poison in order to prove their love for him. After the execution of a member who tried to run away, Jones's followers meekly did what they were told. Forty-five minutes later, Jones revealed that the 'poison' was innocuous. This was the first of a series of suicide rehearsals he called 'white nights'.

New West magazine published an article about Jones's sexual misconduct, using information provided by the Mertles. The article also detailed Grace Stoen's relationship with Jones. By that time, she had fled the Temple and was suing Jones for the custody of her son. In the face of this adversity, Jones came up with plans to build his utopia in Guyana, which he would call Jonestown. He paid $1 million for 27,000 acres of jungle, and in 1977 some 380 cult members headed for Guyana. John-John was among them.

The following year, another 700 members joined them. They were accompanied by as many as 150 children, entrusted to the Temple by the authorities, along with their welfare cheques.

At Jonestown, discipline was tightened. Those who opposed Jones were beaten. Children were treated particularly harshly. News from the outside world was censored. Inmates were told that the Temple was under attack by the CIA and the compound was ringed by armed guards.

Back in the USA, criticism of the cult mounted. Sam Houston, a journalist with the Associated Press, accused the cult of murdering his son. He persuaded Congressman Leo Ryan to investigate.

MURDER OR SUICIDE?

On 17 November 1978 Congressman Ryan, a group of journalists and an NBC film crew flew to Port Kaituma, a small town a few miles away from Jones's base. At Jonestown, their reception was surprisingly friendly. The following morning, however, nine members seized the opportunity to escape from the cult, and another twenty asked Congressman Ryan to help get them out. Under this intensified scrutiny, Jones began to crack.

As the defectors boarded Ryan's plane, a tractor from Jonestown turned up and blocked the runway. On its trailer were twenty armed men who opened fire, killing Ryan, three journalists and one of the defectors.

Back at Jonestown, seated on a crude wooden throne, Jones had bad news for his remaining loyal followers: they were about to die in order to save them from persecution by the authorities. Assured they would 'meet again in another place', the remaining 909 cult members queued up in an orderly fashion to drink Flavor Aid laced with Valium and cyanide.

Mothers gave the cyanide-laced drink to their children.

Infants had it squirted into their mouths from a syringe. Adults calmly drank their poison from paper cups. Then they went out into the fields, lay down and died. When they were all dead, Jones took a pistol and blew his brains out.

16

THUGS

The Murderous Followers of Kali

Kali is the Hindu goddess of destruction and bloodshed. She is the fierce, terrifying incarnation of Devi, the supreme goddess. While Devi's other faces are tranquil and calm, Kali is depicted as a hideous hag, whose face is smeared with blood, with her teeth bared and tongue protruding. She has four hands, which hold a sword, a shield, the severed hand of a giant and a noose. And she is always depicted as naked, except for a necklace of skulls and a belt of severed hands. Often she is shown dancing with the dead body of her husband, Shiva. She inspires bands of murderers and robbers.

Kali is said to have developed her taste for blood when she tried to kill the demon Raktabīja. The problem with trying to kill Raktabīja was that every time a drop of his blood touched the earth, a thousand new demons sprang up. But Kali had a plan. She stabbed Raktabīja with a spear and drank his blood before it could touch the ground.

Like Satan in the West, Kali is associated with the goat and is believed to demand blood sacrifices. At one time in her temple at Vindhyachal in northern India, goats were sacrificed day and night so that rivers of blood cascaded down the steps of the temple and into the Ganges. Supplicants from all over India would make an annual pilgrimage there and flagellate themselves into a state of ecstasy.

But Kali's influence spread far beyond the confines of the temple. Her followers were the Thugs, a secret society of organized criminals who terrorized travellers in northern India for hundreds of years.

Even though their principal activity was strangling travellers and stealing their possessions, Thugs did not consider themselves thieves. Each murder was carried out according to a rigid ritual and the victim was considered to be a sacrifice to the goddess Kali. Strangulation was seen as a holy act, because they believed Kali herself had strangled another demon, Rukt Bij-dana, at the dawn of the world. As she did so, two men were formed from the sweat of her brow and they – and their sons and their son's sons – were sent out into the world to strangle other demons.

A bit like the mafia, Thugs enjoyed the protection of rajahs and rich men, both Muslim and Hindu. They worked in bands and each year they would make a pilgrimage to Vindhyachal to hand over a share of their loot to the temple there. They would then be told by the priests which area they were to work in the following year and were given the blessing of Kali to protect them.

Thugs would seek out a group of travellers and join their caravan. Then, when they considered the omens were right, they would strangle them. To do this, the Thugs would use a *rumal* – a yellow handkerchief with a silver rupee tied up inside it – as a garrotte. The killer would shove his knee deep into the victim's back to hasten his death. The body was then ritually mutilated, before it was buried or thrown down a well. The victim's valuables, along with any attractive children, were taken by the Thugs as they moved on, and everything else was burned. They left no trace except for a secret sign that could be read only by other Thugs.

Thugs maintained that the profit they raised by selling the stolen goods was not their motive for the killing. The killing was done for Kali. Any material benefit to the murderer was due to the munificence of Kali, who provided the Thugs with a living so that they could continue the sacred slaughter in her name.

The son of a Thug would follow his father into the craft, beginning as a scout before progressing to become a grave-digger. After that, he graduated to become an assistant strangler, and then a strangler himself. His first murder would be celebrated as a rite of passage. There would be elaborate ceremonials involving the *kussee*, a sacred pick-axe that every band of Thugs carried. This was said to be a tooth from the mouth of Kali and without it no murder could be sanctified.

Thugs felt no remorse. Killing brought them a sense of elation rather than guilt, and they were proud to have followed in the footsteps of their fathers and grandfathers. One man, who had killed 931 people, told of the joy of outsmarting travellers who were constantly on their guard against Thugs. Befriending and killing the witless victim was an exquisite pleasure, he said. When accused of thieving, he was shocked.

'Thieving? Never,' he said. 'If a banker's treasure were before me and entrusted to my care, though in hunger and dying, I would spurn to steal it. But let a banker go on a journey and I would certainly murder him.'

Thugs had a secret language and sacred groves where their murders were carried out. Victims were buried in a circular pit with the corpses packed tightly around a central core of earth. This prevented jackals from digging up the bodies and the murders being discovered. After each murder, the Thugs would consume a lump of consecrated yellow sugar – or *goor* – which they believed sanctified them.

When the British first came to India, they tolerated the Thugs. It was a local custom and should be respected, they were told. The Indians themselves rarely complained about it: they were far too frightened. The Thugs permeated all levels of society and any complaint was bound to get back to them – with disastrous personal consequences.

When the Thugs were prosecuted they would almost always be acquitted, as local judges were too intimidated to punish them. Thugs could strike in any place, at any time, and no one felt safe from the wrath of Kali. The Thugs boasted that they had a mystical partnership with the tiger, who devoured those who escaped them.

It was estimated that the Thugs killed up to 40,000 people a year. Gangs had up to 300 members and, at particular times of the year, the chances of a traveller completing a journey safely were just one in three. In 1830 one gang murdered 108 people in just three months and an individual Thug boasted more than 1,000 victims.

In 1827 three Thugs turned informer and so four others were charged with murder. But a British judge dismissed the case and charged the informers with giving false evidence. These informers were found guilty and sentenced to five days riding backwards on donkeys around the city of Jubbulpore, followed by five years in jail.

THE SUPPRESSION OF THE THUGS

In 1830 Governor-General Lord William Bentinck decided to put an end to what he called 'the most dreadful and extraordinary secret society in the history of the human race'. He made Captain William Sleeman Superintendent for the Suppression of Thugs. He traced their activities on the most detailed map of India made at that time.

Convicted Thugs were to be branded with the words 'Convicted Thug' on their shoulder and 'Thug' was to be tattooed on their eyelids. Then they would be hanged. Those willing to give information about other Thugs would be spared, but they would never be freed. Many were prepared to speak out, and Sleeman found that Thugs were everywhere. They worked as senior aides to Indian rajahs and as the trusted servants of British officials. Many served in the Indian Army and several worked for British Intelligence.

Soon even the Thugs realized that their goddess Kali was losing the battle with Sleeman and Bentinck. They blamed themselves: Kali had withdrawn her protection because they had neglected her worship.

Sleeman went on to track down the patrons and bankers who had backed the Thugs – he called them 'the capitalists of murder'. Some did not require much persuading when more solid investment opportunities presented themselves. One banker in Omrautee withdrew his funds from the Thugs and invested them instead in the East India Company.

By 1841 the Thugs had been almost entirely stamped out. Several thousand Thugs had been tried and hundreds hanged, and the rest were imprisoned or transported to penal settlements on the Andaman Islands. The less bloodthirsty ex-Thugs were held in Jubbulpore and taught weaving, carpet-making, carpentry and bricklaying. Later, a walled village was built near the jail, where their wives and families could live. Up until the end of the nineteenth century, foreign visitors would come and peer over the wall at the last members of this murderous cult.

17

SEVENTH-DAY ADVENTISTS

The Great Disappointment

The Seventh-Day Adventists are another apocalyptic sect. They came to prominence during the Second Great Awakening, a Protestant religious revival which took place in the early nineteenth century. The church has repeatedly predicted the Second Coming of Jesus Christ and the end of the world and, although they are routinely disappointed, the church has a following of some twenty million people worldwide. Adventists advocate vegetarianism and expect adherence to kosher laws. A prominent adherent of the church was John Harvey Kellogg, who invented cornflakes – which were originally intended to be an aphrodisiac.

Adventism has its roots in the Shakers, a sect officially known as the United Society of Believers in Christ's Second Appearing whose followers believed that Christ would reappear in the 1760s. When Jesus did not show up, a German Lutheran minister named J. G. Bengel got down to some hard numbering work and calculated that Christ would actually return in 1836. Former American Army officer William Miller, however, disagreed with him. From Miller's studies of the Book of Daniel and the Book of Revelation, he computed that the Second Coming would occur on 21 March 1843. He gained thousands of followers.

When Jesus failed to show up again, Miller went back to his

figures to discover that he had made a simple arithmetical error and that he was a year out. It was an easy mistake to make – since there is no Year 0 between the two years, 1 BC and AD 1, which preceded and followed Christ's birth. Taking that into account, Miller predicted that Jesus was going to return to earth on 21 March 1844. With an extra year to recruit new converts, membership of his Church of God swelled to 100,000 people. Many of them sold all their worldly goods and, on 21 March 1844, waited all night out in the open for Jesus's return. But, once again, Christ did not put in an appearance. This was known as the 'Great Disappointment'.

However, the day after the Great Disappointment, one believer named Hiram Edson had a vision. It showed him that Miller's calculations were right, but his interpretation was way off. In fact, 22 October 1844 was the day when God would start 'cleansing the heavenly sanctuary' and separating the sheep from the goats in preparation for the Day of Judgement. How long this cleansing operation would take, no one knew. There was much to do. Once God had got the place spick and span, ready for the righteous to turn up, he would have to go through all the names in the Book of Life and investigate all the sins listed. Only after that would he make his judgement. Then he would send Christ back to earth to separate the righteous from the wicked. In the meantime, those Adventists who had died would be put in a suspended state of 'conditional immortality' until it was decided on the Day of Judgement whether they would either be extinguished along with the wicked or live for ever on earth under Christ's reign.

By December 1844, Ellen G. White was also having visions – although some cynics put those down to her poor mental condition. Her visions – more than 2,000 of them, she claimed – concurred with those of Edson. Her visions carried more weight due to the fact that she was married to the prominent Adventist minister James White, and she began churning out books which extolled healthy living and discouraged the consumption of meat and intoxicants. Virtuous living, she said, would hurry along the Day of Judgement.

Her output was aided by a vision in which God told her that her husband should start a newspaper, *The Present Truth*. In all she wrote over 5,000 articles and forty books covering issues to do with religion, social relationships, prophecy, nutrition, creationism, agriculture, theology, evangelism, the Christian lifestyle, education and health. Following in White's footsteps, follower Rosalie Hurd wrote one of the first books on veganism, *Ten Talents*, which took its title from a quotation from White, who said that the ability to cook was worth 'ten talents'.

The movement settled on the name Seventh-Day Adventists in 1860, when they decided that God could be encouraged to speed up the cleansing process if the Sabbath was celebrated on the seventh day of the week according to their interpretation of the Bible, from sunset on Friday to sunset on Saturday, rather than on the first day – which they believed was Sunday. The organizing body, the General Conference of Seventh-Day Adventists, was set up three years later, and annual camp meetings began in 1868.

Under White's guidance the denomination turned to missionary work. By 1901 it boasted 75,000 members and it oversaw the management of two colleges, a medical school, a dozen academies, twenty-seven hospitals and thirteen publishing houses.

Membership continued to climb, but Seventh-Day Adventist churches were closed down and their property confiscated by the Nazis during the Second World War. Three thousand Adventists were put in prison, where they were tortured and abused. Others were sentenced to death.

'Notwithstanding all these obstacles and difficulties, the work of God made encouraging progress,' said a post-war report. 'Even where the persecution raged, the work went forward. Here workers could not write openly about their activities and about baptisms, all of which was forbidden. Yet they were able to let us know that souls were won for the Lord.'

After the Second World War the Seventh-Day Adventists regrouped, but they still kept their eye on the forthcoming apocalypse. By 1965, it was said that Christ would return before the millennium, but this delay in Jesus's Second Coming led to further disappointment among the church's members.

A dissident Australian former church member, Robert Brinsmead, published *1844 Re-examined*, which cast doubt on the idea that God's judgement of Christians began in 1844. Adventist theologian Desmond Ford also preached along those lines and was expelled from the church.

Early in the new millennium, other Adventist theologians have warned against a new trend, which they call an 'Emerging Church' movement, with its inherently dangerous ideas of 'Spiritual Formulation' (meditative techniques which they see as a feature of New Age religious movements and Catholicism).

'Stay away from non-Biblical spiritual disciplines or methods of spiritual formation that are rooted in mysticism such as contemplative prayer, centering prayer, and the emerging church movement in which they are promoted,' said Ted N. C. Wilson, newly elected President of the Seventh-Day Adventist Church in July 2010. Instead believers should 'look within the Seventh-Day Adventist Church, to humble pastors, evangelists, Biblical scholars, leaders, and departmental directors who can provide evangelistic methods and programs that are based on solid Biblical principles and the Great Controversy theme.'

THE GREAT CONTROVERSY

First published in 1858, *The Great Controversy between Christ and His Angels and Satan and His Angels* by Ellen G. White is a key text that explains the Seventh-Day Adventist understanding of the conflict between God and Satan and also of the Bible and much of world history. It begins with the destruction of Jerusalem in AD 70 and ends with the

Second Coming of Christ, the delivery of God's people, the desolation of the earth and the end of the controversy, during which, after a thousand years, Christ will again return to the earth to resurrect the wicked so that they receive their doom.

At this point the New Jerusalem, in its dazzling splendour, will descend from heaven. Satan will try to take the city and dethrone Christ, only to be defeated. His supporters will see that his cause is lost. His power will be gone and his angels will be unable to prevail against God. Fire and brimstone will rain down on them. For the righteous, raised to heaven in the first resurrection, death will have no power. They will live in peace and there will be no more pain and death.

The book concludes: 'The great controversy is ended. Sin and sinners are no more. The entire universe is clean. One pulse of harmony and gladness beats through the vast creation. From Him who created all, flow life and light and gladness, throughout the realms of illimitable space. From the minutest atom to the greatest world, all things, animate and inanimate, in their unshadowed beauty and perfect joy, declare that God is love.'

18

WICCA

Pagan Witchcraft

Wicca is the revival of what adherents refer to as the 'Old Religion': that is, pagan witchcraft. With no central authority, there is no one to define its beliefs or practices, but followers stress the ascendency of the 'Great Goddess' – sometimes alone, sometimes alongside the 'Great Horned God'. Worship of the Great Goddess follows the cycles of the moon, while worship of the Great Horned God follows the cycles of the sun. Witchcraft and sorcery are also involved in these modes of worship, although Wiccans claim they use only 'white magic', as 'black magic' belongs to Satanists.

The evidence for ancient European cults who practised magic is scant, but witchcraft as it has been known for the last five centuries was the invention of two Dominicans named Jacob Sprenger and Heinrich Kramer, who were sent to Germany during the Inquisition in the fifteenth century to root out heresy. To that end, in 1486 they co-wrote *Malleus Maleficarum – The Hammer of Witchcraft* – in which they described the vile and diabolical practices they had come across, but also outlined what reasons (or excuses) there might be for torturing, mutilating and killing large numbers of women who were accused of being witches. At the time, torture was used to extract confessions from heretics, who were then burned at the stake.

Witches should be treated in the same way as heretics, the book argued.

The founder of the contemporary Pagan religion Wicca was retired civil servant Gerald Gardner. He was a Rosicrucian and had been initiated into Aleister Crowley's Order of Oriental Templars before he discovered a witches' coven in the New Forest in 1939. He said that they let him join in an initiation ceremony where a local woman and practising witch, 'Old Dorothy' Clutterbuck, got him to strip naked. The group, he said, was one of the few surviving covens of the pre-Christian witchcraft sects. He also claimed that they formed a Great Circle that produced a Great Cone of Power that was successful in keeping the Nazis at bay.

Gardner was also into flagellation. This came across strongly in his hand-written *Book of Shadows*, in which he 'recreates' the rituals of witchcraft with elements borrowed from Freemasonry, aspects of Aleister Crowley's beliefs and his own sexual predilections. These practices remain the basis of modern witchcraft, although all of the sadomasochism has been dropped.

Robert Graves gave modern witchcraft another fillip with the 1946 publication of *The White Goddess*, his study of the Moon Goddess in different cultures. Then, in 1951, came the Fraudulent Mediums Act. This effectively repealed all previous Witchcraft Acts and allowed individuals to indulge in any spiritiual practices they liked, provided their activities harmed no one.

Gardner compiled the spells he used in his Bricket Wood Coven in his *Book of Shadows* (something akin to a spiritual diary, which all modern-day Wiccans may compose). In 1952 a young woman named Doreen Valiente wrote to him, asking to be initiated into the craft. Having no objection to ritual nudity (and scourging!), she was initiated into Wicca at midsummer in 1953. Together they revised Gardner's *Book of Shadows*, removing the parts borrowed from Crowley, and in 1954 Gardner published it as *Witchcraft Today*. It claimed that the Knights Templar were initiates of the craft and that fairies were a race of pygmies who had survived alongside their taller counterparts. In 1960 Gardner was even invited to a garden party at Buckingham Palace! In the end, though, Gardner got tired of Wicca and joined the Order of Bards, Ovates and Druids, the brainchild of his friend Ross Nichols.

Many Wiccan groups adhere to the *Charge of the Goddess*, a rather florid statement of their common beliefs, written by Gerald Gardner and Doreen Valiente (although some of it was lifted from *Aradia, or the Gospel of the Witches* by nineteenth-century American folklorist Charles Godfrey Leland). *Charge of the Goddess* evokes the 'Great Mother' and links her to Artemis, Athene, Aphrodite, Diana, Isis and other ancient goddesses. Naturally, Gardner, a naturist, insisted in it, 'Ye shall be naked in your rites'.

When Gardner died in 1964, Alex Sanders and his wife Maxine took over the leadership of the Bricket Wood Coven and popularized their version of witchcraft, which they called Alexandrian Wicca. After Maxine separated from her husband in 1973, she took over the movement and enabled its spread to Australia and America, where other new versions of Wicca sprang up.

One version in particular, the Association of Cymry Wiccae (Welsh Witchcraft), was based at the Church of Y Tylwyth Teg in the American state of Georgia. Its leader was Rhuddlwm ap Gawr, who, in 1965, met one Sarah Llewellyn, and co-created it with her. According to Sarah, in 1271 her distinguished forebear, the Welsh Prince Llewellyn, had commanded his trusted scribes to write down what was left of his family's mystical knowledge. His bard had written this information down in the form of tales in a volume called *The Thirteen Treasures*, which also included bits of knowledge from other Pagan groups and the Knights Templar.

For 700 years the Llewellyn family had kept this knowledge secret, but when Sarah met Gawr she told him all about it. He set up the Church of Y Tylwyth Teg – and the Association of Cymry Wiccae. Their secret mountain base, somewhere in North Georgia, was called Camelot-in-the-Woods and the cult's spiritual training college, the Bangor Institute, taught natural healing, spiritual consciousness and other New Age topics. By the mid-1990s they claimed a total of 15,433 followers throughout the world.

THE CHARGE OF THE GODDESS

Sometimes known as the Charge of the Star Goddess, this is recited during Wiccan rituals:

Whenever ye have need of any thing, once in the month, and better it be when the moon is full, then shall ye assemble in some secret place and adore the spirit of She, who is Queen of all witches. There shall ye assemble, ye who are fain to learn all sorcery, yet have not won its deepest secrets; to these will She teach things that are yet unknown. And ye shall be free from slavery; and as a sign that ye be really free, ye shall be naked in your rites; and ye shall dance, sing, feast, make music and love, all in Her praise. For Hers is the ecstasy of the spirit, and Hers also is joy on earth; for Her law is love unto all beings. Keep pure your highest ideal; strive ever towards it; let naught stop you or turn you aside. For Hers is the secret door which opens upon the land of youth and Hers is the cup of wine of life, and the cauldron of Cerridwen, which is the Holy Grail of immortality. She is the gracious goddess, who gives the gift of joy unto the heart of man. Upon earth, She gave the knowledge of the spirit eternal; and beyond death, She gives peace and freedom, and reunion with those who have gone before. Nor does She demand sacrifice, for behold, She is the mother of all living, and Her love is poured out upon the earth.

She who is the beauty of the green earth, and the white moon among the stars, and the mystery of the waters, and the desire of the heart of man, calls unto thy soul. Arise, and come unto Her. For She is the soul of nature, who gives life to the universe. From Her all things proceed, and unto Her all things must return; and before Her face, beloved of gods and men, let thine innermost divine self be enfolded in the rapture of the infinite. Let Her worship be within the heart that rejoiceth; for behold, all acts of love and pleasure are Her rituals. And therefore let there be beauty and strength, power and compassion, honour and humility, mirth and reverence within you. And thou who thinkest to seek Her, know thy seeking and yearning shall avail thee not unless thou knowest the mystery; that if that which thou seekest thou findest not within thee, then thou wilt never find it without thee. For behold, She has been with thee from the beginning; and She is that which is attained at the end of desire.

THE BRANCH DAVIDIANS

Wacko as Waco

A Bulgarian immigrant to the US, Victor Houteff was a Seventh Day Adventist preacher until 1930 when he was defrocked for heresy. He started his own variation, the Davidians, named after the biblical King David. Houteff claimed he had uncovered a hidden code in the Bible that revealed the prediction of an impending apocalypse and that he had been chosen by God to lead a band of the Elect who would rule the earth alongside Jesus Christ. He set up a school teaching his own interpretation of the scriptures at Mount Carmel, near Waco, Texas.

Houteff died before the last trumpet sounded. Benjamin Roden took over the cult and renamed it the Branch after an apocalyptic verse in the Bible. He wisely avoided setting a date for the Second Coming, and instead churned out religious pamphlets: one, bizarrely, claimed that the Pope had masterminded Watergate.

When Roden died in 1978, his wife, Lois Roden, took over the leadership. Three years later, twenty-three-year-old Vernon Howell joined the cult. He was the illegitimate son of a fourteen-year-old Dallas schoolgirl. He was a slow learner who had dropped out of school in the ninth grade. He failed to develop much physical strength despite his efforts at bodybuilding and fancied himself as a heavy metal guitarist. He begged Lois Roden to let him join the Branch Davidians, claiming he was desperate to join because he was in the grip of a terrible vice: excessive masturbation.

He endeared himself to other members by fixing up the ramshackle ranch buildings at Mount Carmel. And they could not fail to be impressed by his knowledge of the scriptures, as he knew the whole of the New Testament by heart. Two years after he joined, Howell told seventy-year-old Lois Roden that God had decreed that they must conceive a child together and their son would be the last prophet. Though her age precluded any possibility of conception, they became lovers, and this effectively allowed him to take over the cult.

Howell's hellfire-and-damnation sermons sparked new life into the Branch Davidians. The apocalypse was at hand, he said, and they had to cleave to the new prophet. Lois was quickly pushed aside when Howell took a fourteen-year-old bride. He also had sex with other girls in the cult, some as young as twelve.

Lois retaliated by expelling Howell and his offspring from the cult 'unto the tenth generation'. In response, Howell set out with twenty-five members, including most of the youngest ones in the cult, on a trip around the Midwest of America. He moved on to Palestine, where he claimed his status as a prophet was confirmed. He declared he was to fight the world's last great battle again Satan.

He briefly moved to Australia, where he recruited more followers. Upon his return to America, he gathered around him a core of mediocre rock musicians. Like Charles Manson, Howell saw hidden messages from God encoded in rock songs, especially the blues classic 'The House of the Rising Sun'.

Howell moved back to Texas with his sixty-person-strong following. His inner circle included bodybuilders who called themselves the Mighty Men, and at his order they seized control of the Davidian ranch at Waco. In a brief altercation, Lois Roden's son (and successor), George, was shot. Although Howell and his men were charged with the shooting, they were acquitted and went on to fortify the compound at the Waco ranch to prevent Lois

Roden, who had been expelled, from staging a counter-coup. By this time Howell's new Branch Davidians numbered well over a hundred members.

Vernon Howell changed his name to David Koresh, taking the first name from King David and the second from the Hebrew name of the Babylonian King Cyrus, who had allowed exiled Jews to return to Palestine. The ranch at Waco was renamed Ranch Apocalypse, as it was considered the battlefield where Armageddon would begin.

The Branch Davidians were, the newly named David Koresh told them, the Army of God. They lived under martial law. Discipline was rigidly enforced, and any hint of dissent was snuffed out. Koresh took his pick of the wives and daughters of his followers, some of whom were under the age of consent, and slept with them. The other men were denied sex altogether, and were told by Koresh that they were to steel themselves for the battle ahead. While his followers were kept corralled at Ranch Apocalypse, Koresh was amassing a huge arsenal of weapons, including small arms, hand grenades and tactical weapons such as anti-tank guns.

Mark Breault, one of Koresh's original Mighty Men, was not happy about the way things were going. His wife had already left the sect and gone back to Australia. He escaped too, taking with him a detailed diary of his time at Waco. Once away from the sect, he warned the American authorities that Waco was potentially another Jonestown – but it was two years before the authorities got around to doing anything.

The US Bureau of Alcohol, Tobacco and Firearms (ATF) eventually responded to reports of the massive stockpile of arms that the Branch Davidians had accrued. On 28 February 1993 officers from the bureau moved in, concealed in cattle trailers. The operation was supposed to have been secret, but it had somehow been leaked to the media. Upon arriving at the compound, they rushed out of the cattle trucks and were met with gunfire.

The battle lasted just under an hour. Four ATF members were

killed and twenty-four others were wounded. The Davidians lost six. The Federal Bureau of Investigation (FBI) took over the bungled operation and called in hostage negotiators, but they had been trained to deal with fanatics, criminal gangs and politically motivated terrorists – *not* religious groups. Koresh's talk of the Seven Seals from the Book of Revelation was a mystery to them. Despite Koresh telling the FBI that, according to his theology, the Fifth Seal was an enactment of mass suicide, their psychological profilers dismissed this threat. Koresh, they concluded, did not inspire the same fanatical devotion as Jim Jones.

The FBI's conciliatory approach showed some success at first. After a week, two older women and twenty-one children were allowed to leave the compound. But the authorities knew that there were still a hundred people left inside, and at least seventeen of them were children.

As the siege dragged on, psychological tactics were employed. Spotlights were shone through the windows to try to disrupt the cult members' sleep. Loudspeakers blasted the compound with the chanting of Tibetan monks, the screams of dying rabbits and loud rock music. The Davidians countered this by blacking out the windows of the ranch and deadening the sound by piling bales of hay against the walls. Weeks of these tactics brought no results and the new US Attorney General, Janet Reno, who was concerned about the welfare of the children, told President Clinton that she intended to authorize the FBI to use tear-gas to flush out the Davidians.

THE MASSACRE

At 4 a.m. on 19 April 1993, after fifty-one days of siege, two tanks fitted with battering rams rumbled into position outside Ranch Apocalypse. Loudspeakers announced that if the Davidians came out with their hands up, they would not be harmed. Instead the Davidians fired on the advancing tanks. The tanks knocked holes in the walls and pumped in tear-gas. But the Davidians had gas masks to cope with that.

Around midday, FBI officers heard instructions being given to set fires inside the compound. They saw wisps of smoke. Suddenly, the wind whipped across the prairie and turned the ranch into a conflagration. A few members managed to run out of the ranch as its burning watchtower collapsed and the ammunition dump went up in a series of huge explosions.

Eight members of the cult managed to escape the flames, but over a hundred people perished. Twenty-five of the charred bodies belonged to children, twelve of them Koresh's. A two-year-old boy had been stabbed to death and a woman had been shot in the back. Another seventeen members had died of gunshot wounds, five of them children Koresh had shot through the forehead. Koresh himself was apparently shot and killed by one of his own aides, who then turned the gun on himself.

One survivor, Kathryn Schroeder, became a witness for the state and testified that the Davidians had long planned to kill anyone who tried to storm the compound. Murder and conspiracy charges were laid against eleven surviving members of the cult. However, the jury found that the ATF officers had bungled the raid and were largely responsible for the death of their own agents. Five Davidians were found guilty of involuntary manslaughter. Two more were convicted on firearms charges and four walked free.

The faith of the Branch Davidians did not die in the flames at Waco. One member who was away from the ranch during the siege awaited Koresh's resurrection. Another, who lost a son, two daughters and four grandchildren in the conflagration, continued to believe in Koresh's prophecies of the Second Coming. Others believe that the deaths of David Koresh and his followers were avenged in the Oklahoma City bombing, which killed 171 on 19 April 1995, that date being the second anniversary of the end of the siege at Ranch Apocolypse.

20

HARE KRISHNA

Krishna Consciousness

Transcendental Meditation, which involves the repetition of a Sanskrit word or phrase with the aim of achieving inner peace, was made popular in the West by Maharishi Mahesh Yogi in a series of world tours. It became hugely popular in 1967 when the Beatles took up the practice. Members of the band went to meditate with Yogi in India the following year. In the wake of Transcendental Meditation came the International Society for Krishna Consciousness. Devotees with shaven heads and saffron and orange Indian robes paraded the streets, banging drums and chanting the mantra, 'Hare Krishna, Hare Krishna, Krishna Krishna, Hare Hare, Hare Rama, Hare Rama, Rama Rama, Hare Hare.'

Krishna Consciousness was brought to the West by Abhay Charanaravinda Bhaktivedanta Swami Prabhupada. Born Abhay Charan in 1896, he was brought up in Calcutta and educated in English at the Scottish Church College there. Both his father and mother worshipped Krishna, the eighth incarnation of the Supreme Being, Vishnu. They were strict vegetarians and even abstained from drinking tea and coffee. Abhay followed in their footsteps and dedicated himself to Lord Krishna from the age of six. He would eat nothing until he had bathed and worshipped Krishna. At night he would chant Krishna's name while counting on his rosary before going to bed.

His mother wanted him to study to be a lawyer in England, but his father was afraid that if he did so the young Abhay would be seduced by Western ways and start wearing Western clothes, eating meat and chasing women. So Abhay stayed in India and went to work in a chemical plant in Calcutta. In his spare time he devoted himself to the religious life. In the 1920s there was a revival of the Krishna Consciousness movement in India and Abhay became swept up by it. Abhay took as his swami Bhakti-siddhanta Sarasvati – himself a follower of the sixteenth-century Hindu mystic Caitanya Mahaprabhu – who told him to 'print books' and 'carry Krishna consciousness to the West'. Abhay spent his life translating sacred Hindu texts and writing in English on Hindu thought.

His first literary work was an English-language magazine devoted to Krishna Consciousness which he began in his front room in 1944. It was called *Back to the Godhead* and he wrote, designed and published it himself. His scholarship was recognized by the Gaudiya Vaishnava Society, which gave him the title of 'Bhaktivedanta', meaning 'one who has realized that devotional service to the Supreme Lord is the end of all knowledge'.

In 1959 he left his wife and children to become a *sannyasa*, a religious ascetic who relinquishes worldly things to dedicate their life to spiritual pursuits. Because of this, he added 'Swami' to his name and, at the Gaudiya Matha monastery in Allahabad, he produced three volumes of religious commentary.

In 1965 he sailed to America with several boxes of religious books. His lectures attracted a small following in New York and within a year he had initiated eleven disciples into the International Society for Krishna Consciousness. He and his followers vowed to abstain from alcohol, tobacco, drugs, meat, tea, coffee and sex outside marriage.

It was there that he took on the title 'Prabhupada', which is from Sanskrit and means 'he who has taken the shelter of the lotus feet of the Lord'. He was an uncompromising guru. Disciples had to renounce all earthly values to follow the spiritual path. They had to shave their heads and wear saffron and orange robes. They became increasingly visible in America, dancing and chanting 'Hare Krishna' on the streets. They were also known for selling books written by their founder and giving away vegetarian meals.

Prabhupada moved to England and in 1968 established the International Society for Krishna Consciousness's headquarters at a country house near Watford, bought at a knockdown price from ex-Beatle George Harrison. By the time of his death in 1977, more than 200 Krishna Consciousness Centres had sprung up around the world.

Harrison included the 'Hare Krishna' mantra in his 1970 hit 'My Sweet Lord'. He was not the only one of the Beatles to embrace Krishna Consciousness. The 'Hare Krishna' chant also appeared on the Beatles' 1967 track 'I Am the Walrus'. John Lennon included it on the 1969 Plastic Ono Band single 'Give Peace a Chance', as did Ringo Starr on his 1971 single 'It Don't Come Easy'. And Paul McCartney's 1989 single 'This One' featured an image of Krishna riding on a swan on the cover.

The International Society for Krishna Consciousness came under legal investigation after the parents of two Hare Krishna converts claimed that their children had been brainwashed by the sect. But in a landmark ruling in 1976 the Supreme Court of New York found that Hare Krishna had bona fide religious roots and the children of the converts had freely followed the tenets of their chosen faith. In 1989 a similar case was dismissed by the Californian court of appeal, although $75,000 in damages were awarded over the 'wrongful death' of a fifteen-year-old's father who had died, allegedly in part, due to the stress of dealing with the Hare Krishnas.

Before Prabhupada died he set up the International Governing Body Commission to run the Hare Krishna movement. It comprised twenty-nine of his young followers, none of whom had the slightest idea of how to run the multi-million-dollar empire the swami had bequeathed to them. Eleven of them staged a putsch on the unsubstantiated grounds that Prabhupada had authorized their succession on his deathbed. Their leader was Keith Ham, who had taken the name Kirtanananda and ran things from the New Vrindavan, a temple his followers had built in West Virginia. A British breakaway contingent was run by James Immel, who was known as Jayatritha.

Without Prabhupada's restraining hand, disciples began expanding their Krishna Consciousness with LSD. In 1987 Immel was murdered by his follower, John Tiernan, who was probably tripping at the time. Tiernan claimed that he had killed the acid-crazed Immel because he was planning to set up his own personal harem among the female devotees, in contravention of the rules laid down by Prabhupada. Tiernan was convicted of murder and committed to a mental institution.

CHILD ABUSE

In 2002 several of the International Society for Krishna Consciousness's temples in the USA declared themselves bankrupt, after a lawsuit for $400 million was filed in the Texas State Court by victims on charges of abuse (including rape, sexual assault, physical torture and emotional terror), alleged to have occurred in the temples' schools in the 1970s and 1980s. By the end of the 1970s the Hare Krishnas were running eleven schools, known as *gurukulas* or 'houses of the guru', in North America, with several more around the world. Most of these closed down in the 1980s.

It was alleged that children at these schools were forced to sleep in unheated rooms and walk great distances in the cold without coats or shoes. They were deprived of medical care for malaria, hepatitis and broken bones, and scrubbed with steel wool until they bled. Some were moved to other *gurukula* schools in different states without parental consent.

At a meeting in May 1996 ten former Hare Krishna pupils testified that they had been regularly beaten and caned at school, denied medical care, sexually molested and raped at knifepoint.

'I remember being made to sleep naked in a cold bathtub for a month,' recalled Jahnavi Dasi, who was sent to a Krishna boarding school in Los Angeles at the age of four. 'I had wet my bed, and it was easier for them to make me sleep in the tub than to change my sheets.'

Dasi also told the meeting that she wound up in a diabetic coma for three weeks after her teachers insisted that her health problems were a ruse to avoid cleaning the school and chanting in the temple.

In a bid to mitigate adverse publicity, the Hare Krishna movement published in its own official journal a candid exposé of the widespread physical, emotional and sexual abuse suffered by children sent to live in the group's boarding schools. Parents were often unaware of the abuse because they were busy travelling around soliciting donations for the group, leaving their children in the care of monks and young devotees who had no training and often resented the task, the report said.

'We need to get to the bottom of it,' Anuttama Dasa, the North American director of communications for the International Society for Krishna Consciousness said, 'and to the best of our ability do whatever we can to try to repair the damage to the kids and show them we do care as a religious society.'

21

HEAVEN'S GATE

From Suicide to Space

Marshall H. Applewhite, the founder of Heaven's Gate, called his sect 'the cult of cults'. To prove it, he and thirty-eight of his followers, who called themselves angels, committed suicide in March 1997. They were convinced that their bodies were mere containers and that by destroying them, their souls would be released and beamed up to an alien spacecraft that was passing near earth in the wake of Comet Hale–Bopp, which was visible from earth at that time.

The son of a Presbyterian minister, Applewhite had once been a professor of music with a wife and son. But in the early 1970s he had checked into a mental hospital in Houston, Texas, where he asked to be 'cured' of his homosexual feelings. In 1975 he met a psychiatric nurse named Bonnie Lu Nettles and together they set up a cult called Human Individual Metamorphosis (HIM) in California. Applewhite and Nettles claimed to have been sent to earth by spaceship to teach humans how to attain a level of consciousness beyond that available on earth.

At first Applewhite and Nettles supported themselves by stealing cars and successfully undertaking credit-card fraud. They moved back to Texas, where Applewhite took out a full-page advertisement that invited people to join his UFO cult. Those who responded were sent a video showing Applewhite and two apparently stoned followers who appeared to hang on every word that issued from the guru's lips. Followers of the cult were required to give up their names and property and become celibate. Applewhite and some of his senior lieutenants had themselves castrated.

UFO Magazine published a feature on the cult, using the names Total Overcomers Anonymous and Higher Source, which the cult also adopted. In it, Applewhite referred to himself as 'Do' and Nettles as 'Ti'. (It is thought that these names were taken from the names of the notes in the scale ('Do, Re, Mi, Fa, So, La, Ti, Do') of the alien alert notes played in the film *Close Encounters of the Third Kind*. However, others suggest that Applewhite had a special affection for *The Sound of Music*. 'Ti' (or 'Tea') in that film was, like the poison that members of the cult later took, a 'drink with jam and bread, which takes you back to Do'.) Other cult members were called 'Re', 'So' and 'Fa'. The cult outlined its beliefs in a screenplay called *Beyond Human: Return of the Next Level*. The American TV network NBC expressed interest.

The cult moved from Arizona into a $1.3 million mansion in San Diego County that had once been the home of Douglas Fairbanks Junior. This lavish retreat was set amidst three acres of land on a hilltop. When the cult members moved in, however, they had no contact with their millionaire neighbours. They slept on bunk beds, were not allowed to drink or smoke and had to cut off all contact with their families.

To earn money, they designed websites – and to this end the mansion was packed with computers. 'Higher Source is very much "in tune" with the current pulse and future direction of technology,' they boasted on their website. What's more, their leaders 'had worked closely together for over twenty years. During those years each of us has developed a high degree of skill and know-how through personal discipline and concerted effort. We try to stay positive in every circumstance and put the good of a project above any personal concerns or artistic egos. This crew-minded effort, combined with ingenuity and creativity, have [sic] helped us provide advanced solutions.'

One of the cult's clients was the San Diego Polo Club. They asked Higher Source to do some work for them early in 1997, but they received an email saying that Higher Source could not do any work after Easter, as their presence would be needed at an upcoming 'religious festival'.

Cult members wore badges saying they were 'Heaven's Gate Away Team'. They were an 'away team' in the *Star Trek* sense: a group of crew members that has beamed down to the surface of a planet to visit alien life-forms there. Members thought of themselves as being like caterpillars which would eventually make their chrysalises and emerge reborn as butterflies, as they perceived their bodies as vehicles or containers that could be left behind them once their souls had emerged from them. Comet Hale–Bopp was interpreted as 'the sign we've been waiting for'. They believed that following on behind the comet would be 'the spacecraft to take us home'.

Their departure was announced on the internet. 'RED ALERT – Hale–Bopp brings closure to Heaven's Gate,' their home page said. By way of explanation, Applewhite added: 'I am in the same position in today's society as was the One that was in Jesus then … If you want to go to Heaven, I can take you through that gate – it requires everything of you.' The approach of Hale–Bopp meant that his 'twenty-two years of classroom [lessons] here on planet earth [were] finally coming to a conclusion – "graduation" from the Human Evolutionary Level. We are happily prepared to leave "this world" and go with [the spaceship's] crew.'

The website also contained a warning: 'Planet about to be recycled – your only chance to survive – leave with us.'

The cult prepared for their departure by sending videos to former cult members explaining what they were going to do.

'By the time you get this we'll be gone – several dozen of us,' said a note accompanying the videotape. 'We came from the Level Above Human in distant space and we have now exited the bodies that we were wearing for our earthly task, to return to the world from whence we came – task completed.'

'We couldn't be happier about what we're about to do,' said one cult member on the video.

'Maybe they're crazy for all I know,' said a female cultist. 'But I don't have any choice but to go for it, because I've been on this planet for thirty-one years and there's nothing here for me.'

Another female follower, who believed – groundlessly – that Applewhite had terminal cancer, said: 'Once he is gone . . . there is nothing left here on the face of the earth for me . . . no reason to stay a moment longer.'

All thirty-nine of the suicide victims appeared on the tape. They all had their hair cut short, leading the police to believe that they were all young men. In fact, their ages ranged from twenty-six to seventy-two and twenty-one of them were women.

In a second tape, Applewhite gave a long and rambling explanation of their beliefs.

'We came for the express purpose to offer a doorway to the Kingdom of Heaven at the end of this civilization, the end of the millennium,' he said. 'Your only chance to evacuate is to leave with us. I guess we take the prize of being the cult of cults.'

Once the videos had been despatched the thirty-nine members of the cult went out for a final meal in a local restaurant. They then split themselves into three groups and committed suicide in shifts over the next three days. Applewhite had kindly written out suicide instructions for each member: 'Take pudding or apple sauce and mix it with the medicine' – phenobarbitone – 'drink it down with a vodka mixture and relax.'

This was plainly ineffective. Most of the cult members had died of suffocation and two had even suffocated themselves by putting plastic bags over their heads.

One of the farewell videos had been sent to a Beverly Hills businessman who had employed a former member of the cult. The two of them drove to the estate in San Diego indicated in the videotape, where they found thirty-nine bodies lying on their backs 'as if asleep'. They had their hands by their sides and they were each staring at the ceiling through a three-foot square of purple silk, which had been folded into a triangle pointing downwards. They wore identical black slacks and trainers. Their bags had been packed, and they carried identification details in their shirt pockets.

The businessman called the police. The first two deputies who went into the property and who came up close to the bodies had to be rushed to hospital, so a Hazardous Materials team was sent in next to test for poisonous gases. The noxious fumes were discovered to have come from the victims' bodies. These were removed using a refrigerated lorry and a fork-lift truck.

SUICIDE NOTE

Applewhite – 'Do' – left a chilling message for the world on the internet. It began: 'Do's Intro' and a subtitle stated 'What Our Purpose Is – the Simple "Bottom Line"'. It continued as follows:

> Two thousand years ago, a crew of members of the Kingdom of Heaven who are responsible for nurturing 'gardens', determined that a percentage of the human 'plants' of the present civilization of this Garden (earth) had developed enough that some of those bodies might be ready to be used as 'containers' for soul deposits. Upon instruction, a member of the Kingdom of Heaven then left behind His body in that Next Level (similar to putting it in a closet, like a suit of clothes that doesn't need to be worn for a while), came to earth, and moved into (or incarnated into), an adult human body (or 'vehicle') that had been 'prepped' for this particular task. The body that was chosen was called Jesus ...

22

THE ORDER OF
THE SOLAR TEMPLE

The Yuppie Apocalypse

Unlike the People's Temple and the Branch Davidians, the Solar Temple was not an offshoot of a more conventional Christian sect. It claimed its apocalyptic vision derived from the Knights Templar. Formed in 1984, its members believed that, at the Second Coming of Christ, Jesus would appear as a solar god-king. The founders did not encourage drop-outs and hippies to join, favouring instead the attractive, wealthy and influential. One of the most prominent members was Princess Grace of Monaco, perhaps more famously known as the former movie star Grace Kelly. She threatened to expose the Solar Temple as a money-making scam shortly before she died in a car accident. Some fifty of its members lost their lives in a mass suicide in October 1994.

The Solar Temple's founder, Luc Jouret, was born in the Belgian Congo in 1947. After a stretch in the Belgian Army, he studied medicine at Brussels University. He had intended to specialize in obstetrics but he became interested in New Age ideas, especially homeopathy, and, later on, mysticism and the occult. During the 1970s he joined the Renewed Order of the Templars, a neo Nazi organization led by former Gestapo officer Julien Origas.

Soon after Origas's death in 1983 the Renewed Order fell apart in a squabble over finances. Jouret left the sect to form the International Chivalric Order of the Solar Tradition in Switzerland, which peddled a mixture of environmentalism, homeopathy and mysticism. This group soon amalgamated with a cult called the Foundation Golden Way, whose leader, Joseph Di Mambro, believed in a New Age approach to high finance, drawing on metaphysical and mystic knowledge. Together they formed the Solar Temple, a cult that seemed to have the answer to everything in the 1980s.

Jouret was the cult's high priest. He preached that the apocalypse was fast approaching, and that it would come in the form of an ecological disaster. This being the age of the yuppie – the young and upwardly mobile professional – the fees were high and members were served chilled champagne at cult meetings. Jouret recruited new members through his upmarket homeopathic clinic in Geneva. He also toured the world lecturing on environmental politics. This gave him new openings to prominent people.

Instead of employing the heavy-handed discipline used by other sects, Jouret studied all the latest management techniques. He freelanced as a corporate motivator and perfected elegant techniques of control and coercion.

In 1986 Jouret and Di Mambro branched out and formed a Canadian wing of the Solar Temple. They bought an old monastery north of Montreal and started an organic farm there. Meanwhile, Jouret continued to give lectures and seminars on management, motivation and self-realization to large Canadian companies, which gave him plenty of chances to recruit corporate high-fliers. He picked up other recruits by travelling around small towns, giving lectures on homeopathy and whole foods, and he sold inspirational tapes through New Age shops. Using these methods, Jouret managed to lure people such as Robert Ostiguy, the mayor of the town of Richelieu, in Quebec, and

Robert Falardeau, an official in the finance ministry of Quebec, into the Solar Temple.

Membership of the Solar Temple cost $50 a week, and this fee included access to lectures and seminars. For $150 a week, you got the 'Club Arcadia' membership. This enabled – or rather, obliged – members to work at the Temple's organic farm, recruit new members and join in the Temple's religious rites. And for $200 a week, you joined the inner 'Golden Circle'. Members of this upper tier were allowed to join in the Temple's secret, occult rituals. They were also expected to donate all their savings and property to the Temple.

While members of the Solar Temple toiled in the fields producing organic vegetables, Jouret and Di Mambro maintained a playboy lifestyle, travelling the world and skiing. Jouret slowly tightened his grip on the group. He assumed the right to approve marriages and arbitrarily dissolve existing unions. He kept discipline by maintaining that only 100 cult members – the Elect – would survive the impending apocalypse, and Jouret was to decide who those 100 were.

When a disgruntled cult member left in disgust and went to the papers, claiming that they had handed over $500,000 to the sect, details of what was going on in the cult began to come out. Then, in 1993, Jouret was fined $750 on weapons charges. By that time there was growing disquiet in the Canadian branch of the Temple. During the 1980s Di Mambro had invested the Temple's funds heavily in property, but now that market was in decline. The yuppie dream was over and so was its New Age fervour. Soon, Jouret began to talk of mass suicide.

On the night of 5 October 1994, a farmhouse in the farming village of Cheiry, in Switzerland, caught fire. A neighbour raced to the scene and broke into the burning house, where he found the owner, retired businessman Albert Giacobino, shot dead in the bedroom. Firemen searched the farm once they had quenched the flames and they found that the spacious barn had been converted into a temple of sorts. A pentagram had been drawn on the floor. Over a triangular pulpit was a picture of Christ holding a chalice, but the face in the painting was that of Jouret. Around the base of the pulpit, spread out in a sunburst formation, were twenty-three dead bodies: those of ten men, twelve women and Di Mambro's twelve-year-old daughter. The men were wearing robes of white, black and red; the women, white and gold. The cult members seemed to have been well prepared for their send-off. Empty champagne bottles were strewn around the place. Around half of the bodies had plastic bags tied over their faces. Some also had their hands tied together. Others had been shot, up to eight times. Although three rifles were found in the barn, the cult members had been despatched with a .22-calibre pistol. More than fifty shell casings were found on the floor.

Four hours later, and fifty miles away, three chalets in Granges-sur-Salvan had also caught fire. Inside the chalets were twenty-five bodies, five of them children's. The bodies had been badly burned, but plastic residue indicated that they had died with bags over their heads. None had been shot, although some had been badly beaten. The remains of drug paraphernalia indicated that they had been heavily sedated before they were killed. The .22-calibre handgun used in the barn temple at Cheiry was found in the ashes.

Later that same day, an explosion went off in a house in Quebec which was owned by the Solar Temple. In the bedroom, the firemen found the bodies of a man and a woman. Around their necks were medallions showing a double-headed eagle. They were members of the Solar Temple. In the basement they found the bodies of Antonio Dutoit, Di Mambro's Swiss chauffeur, and his British wife, Nicki. Wedged behind the immersion heater was the body of their three-month-old son, Christopher. The child had a plastic bag tied over his head and a stake through his heart. The family had been dead for some time before the fire was started.

Investigators soon discovered the cause of the fire: a crude timer that had been set to ignite cans of petrol. Former cult members claimed that Di Mambro had been annoyed when the Dutoits had had a baby without his permission. The child, Di Mambro said, was the anti-Christ and cult members had been ordered to kill him in a blood-curdling ritual a few days earlier. Jouret and Di Mambro had been seen leaving the house the day before the fire. They had taken a 10 a.m. flight to Geneva in order to finish off the rest of the cult in Switzerland.

At first it was thought that Jouret and Di Mambro had been involved in some financial swindle and had escaped to live a life of luxury with the proceeds. Rumours circulated that they had more than £90 million salted away in a Swiss bank. However, dental records revealed that both Jouret and Di Mambro were among the victims of the fire at the chalets in Granges-sur-Salvan.

They had been telling followers that the cataclysm was imminent for some time and, two days before the murders, Di Mambro took twelve members of the cult out to an expensive restaurant for a last supper. Jouret and Di Mambro believed that, in order to be reborn on a distant planet called Sirius, they had to undergo a fiery death on earth.

In December 1995 sixteen more members of the Solar Temple were found dead near Grenoble, France. And on 23 March 1997 the charred bodies of three women and two men were found in a house owned by a member of the Solar Temple in Saint Casimir, Quebec. They too had burned themselves alive.

GRACE KELLY

One of the cult's most prestigious converts was Princess Grace of Monaco. According to an article that appeared in the *Sunday Times* after her death in 1982, her initiation into the cult involved nude massage and ritual sex. After the ceremony at the priory in the French village of Villie-Morgon, Kelly was asked to donate twenty million Swiss francs to the order. She agreed to pay twelve million francs into a bank in Zurich. Soon, however, she started to have her doubts and threatened to go to the media with lewd stories about the Solar Temple. A few months later, she was out driving with her daughter Stephanie when their car crashed over a mountainside, landing in a garden owned by another Solar Temple member. Kelly was pulled alive from the wreckage, but died in hospital the next day.

23

JEHOVAH'S WITNESSES

Armageddon Next Time

The Jehovah's Witnesses sprang up in the nineteenth century, although the name Jehovah's Witness was not introduced until 1931. The sect is known for its door-to-door preaching, repeatedly inaccurate predictions of the apocalypse and shunning of military service and blood transfusions.

The Jehovah's Witnesses were founded by Charles Taze Russell in 1870. Russell left formal education at the age of eleven and was brought up in a Congregationalist community. He joined the Seventh-Day Adventists, where he came under influence of Jonas Wendel, a man who rejected ideas about the immortal soul, hellfire and that the earth would be destroyed when Christ returned. Instead, Wendel believed that Christ would return the earth to the perfection of the Garden of Eden, where people could live for ever. He believed that the Second Coming would occur in 1873, while Russell set the date as 1874.

When nothing happened in either 1873 or 1874, Russell claimed that Christ had indeed returned, but his presence was invisible. He expounded this view in 1877 in a booklet called *The Object and Manner of the Lord's Return*, but in later editions he sneakily changed the first date of publication on the copyright page back to 1873 and claimed that he had known that Wendel's prediction was mistaken in advance.

He also said that believers would be 'called away bodily' in 1878. When nothing much happened in 1878 he explained that he had meant that believers would go directly to paradise from 1878 onwards, rather than waiting in the grave for the Second Coming like those buried before 1878.

Russell started writing *Zion's Watch Tower and Herald of Christ's Presence* in 1871. In 1881 he established the Zion Watch Tower Bible and Tract Society, which is still the publisher of *Watchtower* and *Awake*, the two magazines that are sold door-to-door by Jehovah's witnesses.

Over the next three decades, Russell wrote six volumes of *Studies in the Scriptures*. Although he maintained that the Bible is the fount of all truth, he asserted that unassisted study was of no use. However, if a student did not read the Bible at all, but read *Studies in the Scriptures* instead, they would still come to enlightenment in two years.

Jehovah's Witnesses seem to have quietly forgotten some of Russell's other claims, though. In 1911 he sold 'Miracle Wheat' seed though the *Watchtower*, at sixty times the price of normal wheat seed. He claimed that it would have a similarly inflated sixty-fold yield, though in court it was shown to be slightly less fertile than ordinary wheat. He claimed under oath to understand Greek, but in court it was shown that he did not know even the Greek alphabet. And a messy divorce showed him to be less morally upright than his followers might have wished.

Russell next claimed that the end of the world would come in 1914. This prediction was based on the dimensions of the Great Pyramid at Giza, despite the fact that they were not precisely known at that time. As 1914 approached, however, the end of the world was delayed to 1915, and then to 1916. The apocalypse has also been expected to occur, according to the prophecies of the Jehovah's Witnesses, in 1920, 1925, 1940, 1975 and 1984.

Since, according to Russell, the world was about to end, there was little point in his appointing a successor. So, when Russell died in 1916, infighting began. The cult was eventually taken over by a New York attorney, Joseph Rutherford, who called himself the 'Judge'. He was almost immediately arrested and sentenced to twenty-five years in prison for opposing America's involvement in the First World War. Jehovah's Witnesses are pacifists, not because they are against killing *per se*, but because they do not think they should take up arms on behalf of earthly governments. After all, Russell had preached that they would fight at Armageddon, where everyone on earth would be wiped out, except for his followers, for whom 144,000 places in paradise had been set aside.

The precise limit Russell had put on the capacity of heaven began to cause problems in the 1930s, when the cumulative total of the cult's followers began to approach that figure. Rutherford, who compiled a seventh volume of *Studies in the Scriptures* in 1917, announced that, once heaven was full, new Witnesses would populate the newly cleansed earth. Rutherford also made another great leap forward in theology. From his luxury home in San Diego, he pronounced that Christ did not die on the cross at all, but at the stake. The Word, he claimed, had been mistranslated.

Jehovah's Witnesses' opposition to conscription caused problems. In America, followers refused to accept any alternative war work on the grounds that enforced civilian work was also conscription. Witnesses suffered badly for taking this stand. Some were beaten up, others tarred and feathered. Many lost their jobs and went to jail. Jehovah's Witnesses made up seventy-five per cent of imprisoned conscientious objectors in the USA.

They were also persecuted in Nazi Germany. Not only did they reject conscription, they refused to give the Nazi salute or acknowledge the swastika. Over fifty per cent of German Witnesses were sent to concentration camps and one in four German Witnesses died during the Nazis' reign.

After Rutherford died in 1942, he was succeeded by Nathan Homer Knorr, who, in 1961, published a new translation of the Bible, the *New World Translation*, to incorporate these departures from the commonly accepted narrative. The following year the Witnesses revised their attitude to secular authority and they adopted an earlier interpretation of Romans 13, which allowed them to obey all civil laws that did not directly clash with God's laws.

In 1966 the Witnesses predicted that the world would end in 1975. When it didn't, membership declined and a few senior members left. Years later, in 2000, the Watch Tower Society split from the powerful governing body of the sect to concentrate on spiritual matters, while also setting up several not-for-profit corporations to deal with administrative matters. The management and workers of these corporations are all Jehovah's Witnesses.

In 2017 the Supreme Court of Russia ruled that Jehovah's Witnesses were an extremist organization, banned its activities in Russia and issued an order to confiscate the organization's assets. Their activities are restricted in many countries.

Even though its prophecies of the end of the world have repeatedly been proved to be inaccurate, the Witnesses' publications continue to point out 'evidence' that the earth is in its final hours and reports a worldwide membership of over eight million people.

JEHOVAH'S WITNESSES AND BLOOD TRANSFUSIONS

Jehovah's Witnesses refuse blood transfusions, including instances when a person stores their own blood for a later transfusion, on the grounds that the Bible prohibits the ingestion of blood. Accepting a blood transfusion is seen as a sin and those who accept one would be shunned by other

Witnesses. Refusing a transfusion makes some operations extremely dangerous and doctors often require Witnesses to sign a waiver to say the doctor was not responsible if anything went wrong.

Many Jehovah's Witnesses carry a card refusing blood donations, thereby releasing doctors from any liability if they die under their care. In some cases, doctors have gone to court to get permission to give blood to Jehovah's Witnesses' children against the wishes of their parents. Cell-free blood products, containing haemoglobin – though not red blood cells – have recently become available and are acceptable to some Jehovah's Witnesses.

In the year 2000, the Witnesses changed the rules on blood transfusions. While their church would no longer take disciplinary action against a Witness who accepted a blood transfusion, it was still to be considered a sin. Disciplinary action had been considered appropriate since those who had accepted a blood transfusion had rejected one of the fundamental tenets of the sect – although they could return to the church if they changed their mind and repented. Furthermore, children who have been administered transfusions against their parents' wishes are no longer rejected or stigmatized.

24

THE RAJNEESH MOVEMENT

The Bhagwan's New Approach to Meditation

Originating in India, the Rajneesh Movement became notorious in America in the 1980s when its commune in Oregon came into conflict, first with local residents, then the authorities. Various legal battles ensued. The cult's leader, Bhagwan Shree Rajneesh, had long been predicting the end of the world and, in 1984, said that two-thirds of the earth's population would be wiped out by AIDS. With the cult in a state of low-level warfare against the authorities, there was a rebellion by his senior staff, who provided evidence of their leader's wrongdoing. Rajneesh was caught fleeing the country, but escaped jail and was deported.

Bhagwan Shree Rajneesh was a new-style Indian guru who did not practise abstinence or asceticism. Born Chandra Mohan Jain to a wealthy middle-class family, he was brought up by his grandparents who spoiled him. Rajneesh was a childhood nickname meaning 'Lord of the Night'.

He was an honours student at the University of Jabalpur, where he went on to become a professor of philosophy. In 1966, however, he left the institution, claiming that he had attained enlightenment without the help of a guru or any rigorous religious discipline. He invented 'dynamic meditation', which involved a catharsis, usually through explosive expressions of anger or even sexual climax. This was one of the many forms of meditation he came up with in his lifetime.

In 1969 he moved the centre of his operations to Bombay, now Mumbai, where he was besieged by young Western drop-outs searching for enlightenment. He took them on as his pupils and, in exchange for everything they owned, gave them lectures and rose-coloured robes. They were encouraged to chant mantras, kick, bite, scream and punch to release pent-up emotions, romp around naked, and have as much sex as they liked.

Rajneesh then took the title 'Bhagwan' – which means 'Master of the Vagina' – and maintained his state of enlightenment with the willing co-operation of a string of young female initiates, some of whose sexual experiences with him were little short of rape, as the guru took it upon himself to teach them the spiritual benefits of sexual submission.

Nude romps on the beach under the auspices of the Bhagwan attracted the hostility of the locals in Bombay, and the cult soon moved to Poona. The Bhagwan's followers took to smuggling drugs to support the organization and the proceeds were funnelled back into the Bhagwan's coffers. When this practice was exposed in a BBC documentary, the Indian authorities began an investigation of the cult's activities. To escape charges of fraud and tax evasion, the Bhagwan moved his operations to Antelope, a small town in Oregon, in America. There he bought a desert property called Big Muddy Ranch for $6 million and renamed it Rajneeshpuram.

While his followers toiled at the ranch in a state of squalor, the Bhagwan lived an opulent lifestyle. He had a fleet of ninety Rolls-Royce cars, four private aircraft, an arsenal of weapons and an endless supply of submissive young women. For his followers, however, the regime grew stricter. They were marshalled by the cult's police force. All elements of individuality were to be stamped out and the outside world, including friends and family, was derided as worthless and meaningless.

Cult members infiltrated the local council and effectively took over the town. Buildings were erected on the ranch without planning permission and, when state officials protested, their offices were fire-bombed. The ensuing FBI investigation uncovered laboratories containing chemical and biological agents on the ranch. Several of the Bhagwan's senior lieutenants – including his personal secretary, Ma Anand Sheela – turned against him and the Bhagwan fled.

He headed for Bermuda, but when his private jet landed at Charlotte Douglas International Airport in Carolina to refuel, he was arrested. Convicted on fraud charges for making false visa applications, he was fined $400,000 and deported. India refused him residence, so he headed to Nepal and then hopped around the globe until 1987 when the Indian government finally let him settle back in Poona.

There followed a time of confusion for his followers. The Bhagwan insisted that he was not a teacher, although his teachings ran to 500 volumes. He started to reject the title of Bhagwan, as some of his acolytes thought that 'Bhagwan' meant 'God', but he insisted he was not God. Now, he told his acolytes, he did not even believe in God. Like Buddha and Lao Tzu, he was an atheist. He was to be known as Gautama the Buddha, he said. Two days later, however, he announced that he was not Gautama the Buddha, but Maitreya the Buddha ('Maitreya' means 'friend'). Two days after that, he declared that he was to be known as Shree Rajneesh Zorba the Buddha, whose zest for life reflected that of the character Zorba the Greek in Nikos Kazantzakis' novel of the same title.

'Zorba the Buddha simply means the synthesis between materialism and spiritualism – that is my contribution,' he explained.

He managed to be Zorba the Buddha for one whole week before he announced: 'Shree Rajneesh is enough to indicate me.'

One month later he became Osho Rajneesh. Osho means 'the whole man'. Seven months later he dropped the name Rajneesh altogether and became simply Osho. All this confusion was brought to a conclusion a few months later, in January 1990, when he died. The cause of his death is unknown.

At the height of his powers, the Bhagwan had run 600 meditation centres around the world. Only twenty were left when he died. The cult, which continued under the name Osho, was taken over by Canadian real-estate magnate Michael William O'Byrne, known to the devout as Swami Prem Jayesh, who turned it into a seemingly harmless 'de-stressing' operation for business executives.

However, two followers of Osho who had clearly been up to no good were Sally-Anne Croft, known as Ma Prem Savita, an accountant from Devon, and Susan Hagan, or Ma Anand Su, an aromatherapist from Hertfordshire. In 1995 they were extradited from England back to Oregon, where they were tried for conspiring to murder a lawyer who had been investigating the goings on at the cult's ranch in Antelope. They were convicted and sentenced to five years' imprisonment.

Nonetheless, other followers continued to proselytize the Bhagwan's Mystic Rose Meditation, which, the Bagwhan turned Osho had claimed was 'the greatest breakthrough in meditation in 2,500 years' and, of all the meditations he had invented, 'perhaps the most essential and fundamental one'.

ATTACKS

During the 1984 Waco County elections, a group of prominent followers of the Bhagwan, led by Osho's second-in-command, Susan Hagan, deliberately contaminated the salad bars in ten local restaurants with Salmonella in an attempt to incapacitate voters for the opposition so that their candidates could win. As a result, 751 people contracted food poisoning. Over one hundred and fifty were violently ill and forty-five were hospitalized. It emerged that the group also planned to contaminate the water system with pathogens they had brought from a medical supply company in Seattle, but in end they changed their tactics and boycotted the elections. Their nefarious methods would have failed anyway, as the locals rightly suspected that the Bhagwan's followers were responsible and retaliated by turning out in unprecedented numbers to vote.

The following year the group planned to assassinate the US Attorney for the District of Oregon, Charles Turner, who was investigating the Salmonella attack. He was also looking into charges of immigration fraud and sham marriages among the Bhagwan's followers. Two of the Bhagwan's followers conspired to murder the attorney and used false IDs to purchase handguns in a different state and stalked Turner, planning to kill him near his office in Portland. Fortunately, however, due to their disorganization, the plot was never carried out and was only uncovered during the legal investigation into the Salmonella attack. Eight of the wrongdoers received sentences, but the Bhagwan himself was never prosecuted as he had been deported and had agreed not to return without the permission of the US Attorney General.

25

THE MORMONS

The Church of Jesus Christ of Latter-Day Saints

The Church of Jesus Christ of Latter-Day Saints, known popularly as the Mormons, was founded in 1830 by Joseph Smith. He was the son of a farming family in the so-called 'burned over' district of New York State. It was 'burned over' because so many evangelists had (figuratively) set fire to the people's hearts there in the early nineteenth century. By the age of fourteen, the young Joseph Smith had been exposed to so much religion that he was deeply confused. He asked God whether he should become a Quaker or an Episcopalian, a Baptist or a Methodist, a Congregationalist or a Unitarian. Which was the one true faith?

In answer to his question, God and Jesus appeared to Smith in a vision and told him that he should join none of these sects. Three years later he had another vision. This time an angel called Moroni told him that there were some golden plates buried in a nearby hillside. Four years later, he dug up the hillside and discovered plates inscribed with what Smith called 'reformed Egyptian hieroglyphics'. He used a pair of 'seer stones' that he called Urim and Thummin to read the script, and they revealed to him Judaeo-Christian scripture about an ancient American civilization.

Smith set to work. He sat behind a curtain and dictated his English translation of the text to his schoolteacher friend Oliver Cowdery. When he had completed the translation, Moroni apparently returned and took the plates away. Then, in 1830, Smith's neighbour and new acolyte, Martin Harris, mortgaged his farm to fund the publication of *The Book of Mormon: Another Testament of Jesus Christ*.

The Book of Mormon tells of three of the lost tribes of Israel and their emigration to America. The prophet Mormon, who had written their story down on the plates, and his son, Moroni, were the last survivors of one of the tribes who had been visited by Jesus after his resurrection. In *The Book of Mormon*, Smith said that the citizens of the United States had to prepare the new Jerusalem in the New World. Christ was coming to rule over the USA for a thousand years.

Initially, things didn't go smoothly. Some contemporaries described Smith as a 'notorious liar'. He was once arrested for fraudulently claiming that he had a special eyepiece that could find buried treasure. Moreover, no one had ever heard of 'reformed Egyptian hieroglyphics'. Smith claimed that Professor Charles Anthon of New York City had confirmed that his translation was accurate, but Professor Anthon himself said that the 'hieroglyphics' he had seen were transparently a hoax, simply a mixture of letters from various alphabets all jumbled up. In fact, Smith's translation also contains passages lifted directly from the King James version of the Bible and a Methodist tract called the *Westminster Confession of Faith*. Smith's defence was, since no one had ever seen this language before, how could anyone judge the accuracy of his translation?

Next, Smith said, John the Baptist had appeared to him and Oliver Cowdery and conferred membership of the Aaronic priesthood (an order of priesthood recognized in the Latter-Day Saints movement) upon both of them. To make doubly sure, the apostles John, James and Peter had also appeared in a vision to ordain

Smith and Cowdery into the Melchizedek order, which had been mentioned in the Book of Genesis. Thus prepared, Smith, Cowdery and four other believers set up the Church of Jesus Christ of Latter-Day Saints.

The church grew quickly, with converts from other strains of primitive fundamentalists, such as the Campbellites. Smith used his swelling congregation as a political powerbase, and this led to violent conflict with their non-Mormon neighbours. In 1839 the church, now 10,000-people strong, moved to Kirkwood, Ohio, where Smith set up the first Mormon temple. He went on to open temples in Independence, Missouri, and in Nauvoo, Illinois, and numbers continued to swell, with some 5,000 converts coming over from England.

Non-Mormon residents of Nauvoo were not happy about the appropriation of their town, particularly when Smith took over as mayor, commanding officer of the local militia and editor of the local newspaper. There was also dissent within the church, with former Campbellites becoming concerned about the rituals Smith was introducing. Others started to have their doubts when Smith began practising polygamy. It was said that he had up to eighty wives, but Smith justified this by claiming that Jesus Christ had not just one wife, but three: Mary of Bethany, Mary Magdalene and Martha, and Abraham, Isaac, David and other Old Testament figures seemed to have had had lots of wives, too.

Some dissenters left the church and set up their own rival organization and newspaper, but Smith ordered his followers to burn their paper and smash their presses. In the resulting furore, Smith and his brother Hyrum were jailed. The jail was stormed by an angry mob of dissenters who shot and killed Smith and his brother.

Smith's unexpected death led to a power struggle within the church. Brigham Young, another polygamist, took over and the church split into three groups: two who remained in Illinois and Missouri, and the other – Young's new wing – trekked off through Nebraska and Iowa to what is now Utah, where they set up their own territorial government and judicial system. Later on, this wing of the church sent missionaries around the world and some 100,000 converts poured into Utah, mainly from Britain and Scandinavia.

Soon, however, the authority of the USA's federal government slowly began encroaching upon the Mormons. In 1862 the American Congress passed the Anti-Bigamy Act, which outlawed polygamy. Mormons were arrested and fined for this practice. The Edmunds–Tucker Act of 1887 dissolved the church as a legal entity and confiscated over $50,000 worth of property. The church realized it would face total destruction if it did not adhere to the new laws. In 1890, it officially suspended polygamy, though many Mormons privately continue the practice.

The Mormons who remained in Illinois, including Smith's widow, Emma, formed the Reorganized Church of Jesus Christ of Latter-Day Saints under the leadership of Smith's son, Joseph III Junior (Joseph Smith's father had also been called Joseph). They are now based in Kirkwood, Ohio, and do not practise polygamy.

The Church of Christ (Temple Lot) stayed behind in Independence, Missouri, which Joseph Smith once said would be the site of the New Zion when Christ returned. They are against polygamy too.

OTHER FAITHS

Mormons believe that God's plan for salvation includes non-believers and believers, as well as those who have never heard of Jesus Christ. Members of other faiths will have the chance to learn the true gospel of Jesus Christ after their earthly deaths. Believers of other faiths will also have the chance to accept or reject the covenants and ordinances of salvation performed for them by proxy on earth.

In 1978 the Church's First Presidency issued a statement that:

All human beings are children of God and therefore brothers and sisters.

The only way to obtain a fullness of joy is through the gospel as restored to the Church of Jesus Christ of Latter-Day Saints.

Everyone will have the opportunity to accept the gospel, if not in mortality, then in the life to come.

Great religious leaders of the world received part of 'a portion of God's light'.

These leaders and others were given moral truths by God 'to enlighten whole nations and to bring a higher level of understanding to individuals'.

26

ZOROASTRIANISM

The Temple Fire

Zoroastrianism is the pre-Islamic religion of ancient Iran. Following the Arab invasion in the seventh century BC and the introduction of Islam, Zoroastrians were persecuted. Many converted to Islam. Between the eighth and tenth centuries others migrated to Gujarat, where they were given refuge and became known as 'Parsis' – the Gujarati for Persians. They worship in fire temples where a fire is kept burning on the altar. Westerners mistakenly believed they worshipped fire, but the fire symbolizes God's light or wisdom. In modern-day Islamic Iran, fireworks are set off to celebrate Nowruz, the Zoroastrian New Year, at the spring equinox.

The prophet Zoroaster was born to the Spitama clan in what is now north-east Iraq or south-west Afghanistan, at a date around 1,500 to 1,000 BC. Zoroaster is the Greek rendering of the name Zarathustra. He is known as Zarathusti in Persian and Zaratosht in Gujarati.

Zoroaster began his training to be a priest at seven years old, and at twenty he left home to travel and continue his studies. He is thought to have been a family man, as he had three wives, three sons and three daughters. As a result, most Zoroastrian worship happens in the family home. There is no tradition of monasticism or celibacy in Zoroastrianism.

At the age of thirty, during a spring festival, he had a vision of a shining being who introduced himself as Vohu Manah – 'Good Purpose' – and taught Zoroaster about Ahura Mazda, who was the omniscient, omnipotent and omnipresent creator of life and the source of all happiness. He was surrounded by the Amesha Spentas or 'Holy Immortals' who emanated from him like rays of light. These were Asha Vahishta, truth and righteousness; Spenta Ameraiti, 'holy devotion, serenity and loving kindness'; Khashathra Vairya, 'power and just rule'; Hauravatat, 'wholeness and health'; and Ameretat, 'long life and immortality'.

Zoroaster embraced Ahura Mazda and rejected the religion that he was born into (one loosely based on a form of Hinduism, which promoted the worship of many gods), along with its kind of caste system, the sacrifice of animals, a rigid form of worship and the use of intoxicants in its ritual as well. Instead, he propounded the ideas of free will, individual judgement, heaven and hell, the resurrection of the body, the Last Judgement and everlasting life after the soul and the body were reunited.

At forty-two, he received the patronage of Queen Hutaosa of Persia and a ruler named Vishtaspa and established a community of followers. He died at the age of seventy-seven and is thought by some that he was murdered by a priest of the religion he was born into.

Zoroaster had rejected the religion of Bronze Age Iran, along with its many gods. He believed that there was only one God: Ahura Mazda, or the 'Wise Lord'. Ahura had two sons, Spenta Mainyu, the 'Bounteous Spirit' who chose the way of goodness, truth and justice, and Angra Mainya, the 'Destructive Spirit' who chose evil, injustice, destruction and death.

Through Spenta Mainyu, God had created a world that was pure, but it was constantly under attack by Angra Mainyu, who inflicted natural disasters, famine, sickness, ageing and death upon the world. The result was cosmic dualism: light and darkness, life and death. Existence was a mixture of these two opposing forces, wherein one could not be understood without the other.

This conflict also produced a moral dualism where human beings could either decide to follow the path of *asha*, or truth, which led to peace and everlasting happiness in heaven, or the path of *druj*, or deceit, which led to misery, degradation and hell. Modern Zoroastrians believe that goodness will ultimately triumph over evil, and when mankind finally chooses good over evil there will be paradise on earth and the souls of the dead – initially banished into the outer 'darkness' – will be revived. To this end, Zoroastrians dedicate themselves to improving their communities, giving generously to charity and promoting educational and social initiatives.

Zoroastrians pray several times a day, sometimes wearing the *sudreh*, a long white shirt, and the *kusti*, a cord tied round it, given to them at the Navote initiation ceremony held when they are between the ages of seven and twelve. The *kusti* is tied around the *sudreh* three times to remind them of the threefold religious maxim: 'Good thoughts, good words, good deeds'. The ceremony is performed by a *mobed*, a Zoroastrian priest. A Zoroastrian child would have already learned their daily prayers and to purify themselves with ritual washing.

All Zoroastrian ceremonies and rituals take place in the presence of sacred fire, as it is seen as the supreme symbol of purity, and representative of the light of God and the illuminated mind. The fire in their temples is never extinguished.

Zoroastrian sacred texts are collected in the *Avesta*. The core of it is formed by seventeen poems, or Gathas, which are thought to have been written by Zoroaster himself in an ancient dialect now difficult to understand, in which he addresses Ahura Mazda himself, taking the opportunity to outline the Wise Lord's doctrines. In one, he writes:

I shall recognize Thee as strong and holy, Ahura Mazda, when Thou wilt help me by the hand with which Thou holdest the recompenses that Thou wilt give, through the heat of Thy truth-strong fire, to the wicked man and the just – and when the might of Good Purpose shall come to me.

Then as holy I have recognized Thee, Ahura Mazda, when I saw Thee as First at the birth of life, when Thou didst appoint rewards for acts and words, bad for the bad, a good recompense for the good, by Thy innate virtue, at the final turning point of the creation.

Along with these poems and other early works of scripture, there are also more recent commentaries, along with myths, stories and details of rituals which shape the Zoroastrian religion.

ZOROASTRIANISM TODAY

In 2019 there were 167 fire temples in the world: 45 in Mumbai, 105 in the rest of India, and 17 in other countries. Once one of the most powerful religions in the world, there are now thought to be fewer than 200,000 Zoroastrians in the twenty-first century. Census data is not up to date, but it is thought that there are around 70,000 Zoroastrians in India, fewer than 1,700 in Pakistan and around 25,000 in Iran. In the face of Islamic State violence, up to 100,000 Iraqi Kurds gave up Islam and converted to Zoroastrianism. There are 3,500 Zoroastrians in Australia and some 15,000 in the US. Freddie Mercury was a Parsi and identified as a Persian, though his parents came from India.

In the Zoroastrian year, there are seven obligatory feasts, six of which are: *Maidyozarem*, the 'mid-spring' feast; *Maidyoshahem*, the 'mid-summer' feast; *Paitishahem*, the feast of 'bringing in the harvest'; *Ayathrem*, the feast of 'bringing home the herds'; *Maidyarem*, the 'mid-year' or winter feast; and *Hamaspathmaidyem*, the feast of 'All Souls'. Their origins lie with the agricultural people of the Iranian plateau and relate to the changing seasons. These are communal celebrations with feasting and merry-making. The most important festival of all is *Khordad Sal*, the putative day of birth of Zoroaster. It is celebrated with prayers in the fire temples and feasting.

27

ANOTHER 'FAMILY'

The Messiah Who Stole Children

While Charles Manson's 'Family' was terrorizing California, another equally bizarre cult was flourishing in Australia. Also known as the Family, it was founded by Anne Hamilton-Byrne, who claimed to be the reincarnation of Jesus Christ. She kidnapped children, gave them her surname, dressed them alike, bleached their hair blond so that they appeared to be siblings, and dosed them with LSD and other psychoactive drugs. She taught them to believe that they were to inherit the earth after a forthcoming apocalypse. When one of the daughters was expelled from the cult, she discovered that she was not Hamilton-Byrne's biological daughter and went to the police. The cult was raided and the children freed.

In the 1960s there was widespread interest in mysticism. LSD and other drugs were thought to provide easy access to mystical experiences. People were eager to throw off the constraints of the conventional family structure and experiment with alternative ways of life. What made Anne Hamilton-Byrne's Family different was that its recruits were not consenting adults seeking novel ways of living, but children recruited by deception and held captive.

Hamilton-Byrne was born Evelyn Edwards in the town of Sale, in Victoria, Australia in 1921. She was one of seven children and spent time in the Old Melbourne Orphanage, as her mother was mentally ill and her father itinerant. Among the stories she told was that her mother was a direct descendant of the French royal family and a member of the Scottish Hamilton clan, while she also claimed her father was Lawrence of Arabia and had a big castle in Germany. Her mother, who claimed to be a medium and psychic, spent twenty-seven years in mental hospitals and died in one. Of her father, the orphanage's records merely notes: 'Whereabouts unknown'.

At the beginning of the Second World War, Evelyn's father joined the army, stating his religion as Methodist. When he was discharged on the grounds of ill health in 1944 he was listed as a 'spiritualist', but Evelyn maintained that he was a Buddhist. After the war, she claimed that her parents went to India to seek enlightenment at an ashram founded by Nobel Prize winner Rabindranath Tagore. She also claimed that her father was a friend of the British millionaire and philanthropist Lord Nuffield, while her mother had a Tibetan guru and could travel outside her body.

When Evelyn was twenty she married Lionel Harris, an Royal Australian Air Force policeman. They had a daughter named Judith who later called herself Natasha. But after Lionel died in a car accident in 1955, she started calling herself Anne Harris. Later, in 1959, she enrolled in a yoga class in Melbourne as Anne Hamilton. The following year the Gita School of Yoga opened in Melbourne and Anne began to teach there, introducing herself as a psychotherapist and nurse. She used her yoga classes to recruit followers, targeting in particular wealthy Jewish women who were going through a perceived midlife crisis. Anne believed that if she could get them to leave their husbands and turn their backs on their families, they would be hers for life.

Anne left the Gita School of Yoga after casting a 'spell' on a student who then fell ill. In 1965 she married a former navy officer named Michael Riley and went to live with him in the Dandenong Ranges outside Melbourne. The marriage did not last long, but in that time Riley put Anne in contact with someone who would go on to become a vital member of the Family. This was Dr Raynor Johnson, an English physicist Riley did gardening for, who, in his sixties, had become in interested in religion and Eastern mysticism.

Anne visited Johnson three days before Christmas in 1962. She said she understood that he was about to visit India, and he thought she was a clairvoyant. In fact, she had been study-ing her subject closely. After meeting his wife Mary, Anne predicted that she would become dangerously ill on the trip and, indeed, Mary came down with dysentery in India. This convinced Johnson that Anne was the Messiah she claimed to be and he adopted the role of John the Baptist to her Jesus. Others in the inner circle were seen as reincarnations of the Apostles. She told them that the world would end in 1983 and they should prepare themselves.

She began to hold meetings on Thursdays and Sundays at John-son's home, Ferny Creek, wherein she would discuss the principles of yoga and meditation. There they built the Santiniketan Lodge, which was named after Rabindranath Tagore's ashram in India. This was where the Family, or the Great White Brotherhood, was formed.

One of the cult members was Marion Villimek, who ran the Newhaven Hospital in a suburb of Melbourne where patients were treated with the hallucinogenic drug LSD. Psychiatrists and patients were recruited to the sect.

Things took a darker turn between 1971 and 1975, by which time Anne had acquired fourteen children and infants. Some were taken from Family members, others were obtained by irregular adoption procedures arranged by social workers, doctors and lawyers under her influence. Their surnames were changed to Hamilton – later Hamilton-Byrne after Anne married William Byrne in 1978 – by deed poll or on forged birth certificates. Dressed identically, with uniform blond hair, they were told that they were Anne's biological children while other Family members were informed they were the result of a breeding process. The women who looked after them were referred to as aunties.

These children were held in seclusion in Kai Lama, near the town of Eildon, Victoria. They were allowed no contact with the outside world and were disciplined with savage beatings and starvation diets. Co-operation was ensured by virtue of a range of psychoactive drugs. On reaching adolescence they underwent an initiation that involved being dosed with LSD and left in a dark room, which caused some of them psychological damage. The children were further indoctrinated by visits to gurus in the US and India. Meanwhile Anne and Bill Hamilton-Byrne grew rich from donations provided by wealthy adherents.

At the age of seventeen, Sarah Hamilton-Byrne seemingly became troublesome and rebellious, and was expelled. She came to the attention of a private detective investigating the sect and, with his assistance, discovered that she was not really Anne Hamilton-Byrne's child. They went to the police.

In 1987 Kai Lama was raided and the children were taken into care. Some of the 'aunties' of the Family provided information about their faked adoptions and were eventually convicted of obtaining money from the Department of Social Security by fraud. The Family's solicitor also confessed to forging birth records.

The cult had properties abroad and Anne Hamilton-Byrne and her husband managed to remain beyond the reach of Australian law in the UK and US. But in 1993 they were arrested by the FBI and extradited to Australia, where they were charged with conspiracy to defraud and to commit perjury by falsely registering the births of three children as their own. They pleaded guilty to the lesser charge and were fined $5,000 each. They also paid compensation to victims in civil law suits.

Bill Hamilton-Byrne died in 2004 and Anne succumbed to dementia. Under the name Sarah Moore, the rebellious, falsely adopted daughter who had pulled the plug on the Family, wrote

Unseen, Unheard, Unknown, her account of life inside the cult. The documentary *The Family* was released at the Melbourne International Film Festival in 2016.

LSD

Lysergic acid diethylamide (LSD), also known as acid, was synthesized by the Swiss chemist Albert Hoffman in 1938 and was found to be hallucinogenic. It altered the user's state of consciousness, making them see or hear things that did not exist. Users often felt that it brought them into contact with the spiritual and cosmic order. It can precipitate psychosis in those with a family history of schizophrenia, though at one time it was used to treat the condition. Harvard psychologist Timothy Leary promoted its recreational use with his dictum 'Turn on, tune in, drop out' and it became a cornerstone of 1960s' counterculture.

In 1971 the United Nations Convention of Psychotropic Substances required its prohibition by all signatories. These included the United States, Australia, New Zealand, the UK and most of Europe.

28

THE GNOSTICS, THE WALDENSIANS AND THE CATHARS

The Persecution of Heretics

I n AD 325 the Emperor Constantine called upon the Council of Nicaea to hammer out what the set of core beliefs for Christians were: their most notable conclusion was that of the deity of Christ (and not of other gods). After Constantine had decreed that Christianity was the state religion, Gnostics found that they were liable to be persecuted for heresy, as they took their name from the Greek word for 'knowledge' and their ideology was a mixture of Christian ideas, Platonic philosophy and Zoroastrian belief (in particular, that the world was made up of opposing forces – light and dark, good and evil, spirit and matter).

Gnostics believed that humans were spiritual beings forced to dwell in the material world. They thought that once people had the essential '*gnosis*' (knowledge) given to them by Christ, they could discover the ideal world inhabited by God. Some believed that a state of ecstasy would provide this divine illumination. Others believed that you could only get there the hard way, through fasting and meditation.

Gnosticism soon became riven with sects. One of the more extreme was that of the Manichaeans, who followed the third-century heretic Mani – whose name has given us the word 'maniac'.

Mani's followers practised extreme asceticism. They were forbidden to kill any animal or plant for food and, if possible, not even to break a single twig. Mani went to India and China to spread his beliefs, but when he got back the new king, Bahram I, arrested him. Mani was then crucified and his corpse flayed.

When the persecution of the Gnostics began, they became a secret sect and employed passwords, secret signs and handshakes to safely identify other members. By AD 500, however, Gnosticism disappeared completely. We only know what its followers believed because twelve leather-bound books of their writings were discovered in a cave in Egypt in 1945. The books narrowly escaped destruction after the mother of the two boys who had discovered them began using them to light her stove. Even when the content of the books was revealed, wider knowledge of their existence was suppressed for decades by the Catholic church, who found their doctrines dangerous.

Many centuries after the Council of Nicaea, the great theologian St Augustine, Bishop of Hippo, defined the central tenets of Christianity. As a youth, Augustine had been a practitioner of Manichaeism and later he became a Manichaean. They were a sect who condemned the Christian doctrine of the trinity (three gods in one), as it seemed to them to imply that there were three separate gods.

Later on in his life, Augustine accepted the Christian idea of the trinity, but went on to attack a then new set of religious beliefs which went by the name of Pelagianism. Its founder, Pelagius, was a Celtic monk who held that it was possible for a man, with a great deal of effort, to live a sinless life. This was not so, Augustine said. Everyone – even newborn babies – was tainted with the original sin bequeathed to us by Adam. After all, he avowed, children were produced by sexual intercourse, which was sinful.

This battle raged on for centuries. Eventually, Augustine's line of argument won. However, this left Christian theologians with another problem: how could Christ have been born without sin?

By the twelfth century the doctrine of the Christian church was more or less settled. The issue now lay with the fact that most people were illiterate and could not read the Bible. Services were conducted in Latin, which few of the congregation could understand. And yet, they could see that their church was corrupt. The clergy lived a life of luxury, often cohabiting openly with their mistresses (as ecclesiastical marriage had recently been banned).

In 1176 a wealthy French merchant called Peter Waldo decided to clean things up. He was even given a dispensation to preach by the Pope, provided that he obtained a licence to do so from his local bishop. However, since the Bishop of Lyons was one of the fat cats Waldo wanted to denounce, his licence was refused and, in 1184, Waldo and his followers were excommunicated.

The Waldensians became evangelical ascetics and went on the road. Over the years, they became more radical. They rejected established ideas of purgatory, transubstantiation (that the bread and wine at a mass turned into the actual body and blood of Christ), the invocation of God as in 'in the name of the Father', excommunication, confession, absolution, penance and the sale of indulgences. They celebrated baptism, marriage and the Eucharist – the latter only once a year, on the Thursday before Easter. They translated the Bible into French and allowed women into the ministry. The so-called Waldensian 'heresy' proved so popular that, in order to counter it, Pope Innocent III formed the Poor Catholics, which aped the popularism of Waldensian ideas while staying within the edicts of the Catholic church.

When that did not work, the Catholic church resorted to persecution. Waldensians were imprisoned and burned as heretics. Augustine had already ruled that it was perfectly acceptable to use force to save people from heresy. After all, you might burn their body, but you would save their immortal soul. Waldensian cells survived in remote settlements in the Alps, however, and by the sixteenth century there were enough surviving Waldesians to form an alliance with their natural heirs, the Calvinists.

During the twelfth century the crusades were in full swing. Travel between East and West increased enormously and ideas long suppressed in Europe began to surface again. Among them was Manichaeism.

This flourished in and around the city of Albi in south-west France, before spreading to Italy, Spain and Flanders. The cult's followers were called *Cathari*, or Cathars, which means 'pure ones'. The Cathars were also known as Albigensians, as there were many adherents of this sect in the city of Albi and the surrounding area during the twelfth and thirteenth centuries.

The Cathars took Zoroastrian dualism to its extremes. They believed that the material world existed on the dark, evil side of the universe, and so Jesus Christ, who existed on the good side, could not have been born into it. Consequently, he could not have been crucified, so the cross had no significance. The trappings of the church existed in the material world as well, so the Cathars eschewed those too.

The human soul belonged on the good side of the universe, but it was trapped on the bad side by being housed in the body. Consequently, the Cathars were against marriage, sex, eating meat, drinking wine or doing anything else that brought material comfort or pleasure (though they did eat fish in the mistaken belief that fish did not multiply by copulation). Believers were not required to hold too fast to this. But complete abstinence was required of the Perfecti who formed the inner circle of the church.

Fearing persecution, the Cathars kept their faith secret. When the Pope found out about it, he sent Cistercian monks to try and bring followers back into the Christian fold. But the Cistercians met with little success and were mocked in the streets of Toulouse. Count Raymond VI of Toulouse, who controlled the Cathar regions of southern France, was himself a believer. Pope Innocent III sent an envoy to the count, but the envoy was assassinated. The Pope responded by ordering a crusade to be held against the Cathars, the first in Europe.

THE ALBIGENSIAN CRUSADE

In 1208, 20,000 knights under Simon de Monfort attacked the town of Béziers. When soldiers asked the papal legate, Arnaud, Abbot of Cîteaux, how they could distinguish between a Cathar and a good Catholic, Arnaud replied: 'Kill them all; God will know his own.' So they did.

But the slaughter of the entire population of Béziers only sharpened the Cathars' resolve. They fought on for another forty years. And for those who believed that the world was an evil place, death held little fear. Many Cathars performed the rite of Endura, a sanctified form of suicide through fasting. Perfecti who were given the choice between converting to Catholicism or burning for their beliefs chose martyrdom.

The Cathars' last stronghold was the fortress of Montségur in the Pyrenees. Thought to harbour sacred Christian treasures, including the Holy Grail, it came under repeated attack. In March 1244, after a ten-month siege, the Cathars surrendered. Two hundred men and women walked out of the fortress, singing, straight into the massive funeral pyres the crusaders had prepared for them. Afterwards, no treasure was found in their deserted fortress.

Hidden cells of Cathars continued to worship in secret for another fifty years. Some fled to the Balkans, where they continued to follow their beliefs until the fifteenth century, when the last members of the Cathars died or were finally converted to Islam.

29

KHLYSTY

New Christs

Khlysty was a sect of the Russian Orthodox Church. Devotees used to see themselves as reincarnations of Christ, but they were nicknamed the 'Khlysty' from the word 'Khlyst', which is the Russian for a 'whip' or, in other words, a flagellant. The Khlysty practised ecstatic dancing and were thought to have held orgies. They were persecuted by the authorities, but secretly supported by the nuns of the Ivanoskii cloisters in Moscow and many merchants. One adherent was Grigori Rasputin, who was introduced to the sect as a teenager and followed its precepts for the rest of his life.

About three centuries earlier, in 1645, a young peasant named Danil Filippovic, after shunning conscription on the grounds of Christ's own pacifism, had a revelation. He threw his entire religious library into the Volga River and told the crowd gathered around him that the holy religion had lost its purity some 300 years earlier and that the Antichrist had arisen from among the monastic order of the Orthodox Church. On Mount Gorodin, in Vladimir province, a hundred miles east of Moscow, the crowd raised their hands to the sky and begged the god to descend. Danil said the Lord of Hosts came down from the clouds and inhabited his body.

Filippovic became a 'living god' and came up with twelve commandments:

> I am God, foretold by prophets, who descended to earth for the salvation of the souls of humanity. There is no God other than myself.
>
> There is no other teaching. Do not seek another.
>
> Upon what you have been founded, stand therein.
>
> Drink nothing intoxicating.
>
> Do not commit any sin against your body.
>
> Do not marry; and whoever is married, live with your wife as though she was your sister.
>
> Do not speak any profanity or vulgarity.
>
> Do not attend weddings or child baptism [of the Russian Orthodox Church], and do not patronize any place where alcohol is served.
>
> Do not steal. Whoever steals even one kopek, this will serve as evidence for his sentence to burn in the fire of hell until it is finally exhausted. Only then will he acquire forgiveness.
>
> Retain these commandments in secret; do not declare them either to father or mother. If you are beaten with a stick or burned, endure it. Whoever endures [persecution] will be faithful and receive the heavenly kingdom, and while on earth will receive spiritual strength.
>
> Visit one another; be hospitable with bread and salt; show loving kindness to each other. Observe my commandments.
>
> Believe in the Holy Spirit.

The resulting Khristovshin ('Christ Community') Movement attracted followers both rich and poor. Filippovic chose Ivan Timofeevich Suslov to be his spiritual son –a replacement for Jesus – and Suslov's wife became the first 'Theotokos', or 'mother of Jesus'. Filippovic also appointed twelve apostles.

Suslov moved to Moscow, where he was arrested – apparently

arbitrarily. Upon his release in 1658, he established four houses of worship – known as 'arks' – and converted several monks, who also became known as Christs, like everyone else in the sect. Suslov died in 1716 and was buried at the Nikolski Church. He was later exhumed and interred in the Ivanovskii Convent, under a tombstone bearing the inscription: 'Here is buried a saint pleasing to God.'

After Suslov's death, the sect was taken over by Prokopi Danilov Lupkin, a deserter from the Royal Guard. In 1717 a persecution of the Khlysty began, with adherents arrested and beaten. The persecutions continued after Lupkin's death in 1733, but by this time converts were beheaded rather than beaten. Others were whipped and exiled to the Perm province in the Ural Mountains.

In 1740 a new 'Christ' named Andrei Petrov was appointed as head of the movement in Moscow. Under his leadership, the sect rapidly expanded again, but this in turn attracted further persecution, with some followers being burned at the stake, hanged or beheaded. Nevertheless, the sect continued to find new Christs, but it was forced to go underground.

Although these Christs were ascetic puritans who abstained from meat, alcohol and tobacco, lurid tales circulated about their practices. They were rumoured to practise infanticide and cannibalism in their secret meetings. It was said that Black masses were performed on the body of a naked woman they called the 'bogoroditsa' ('bearer of god') whose child had been sacrificed.

In addition, the Khristovshin thought that believers could not been forgiven unless they had sinned. The easiest way to do that, they found, was to satisfy their carnal desires. They practised the rite of 'lucerna extincta', which involved men and women meeting at night, extinguishing any light and having intercourse. Allegedly, the couplings were sometimes incestuous.

Their ceremonial rites included self-flagellation and frantic dervish-like dancing. After the dispersion of holy water, men and women would rotate in different directions before gathering in opposite corners of the room and clashing into one another forty or fifty times. Eventually, they dropped down exhausted and proffered prophecies. Then an orgy would ensue. It was whispered that the resulting illegitimate children would be sacrificed and their blood used in the Eucharist, and that those wishing not to take part had castrated themselves. Of course, these accounts may have been exaggerated or even made up by their persecutors.

GRIGORI RASPUTIN

Born Grigori Yefimovich Novykh in Siberia in 1869, his licentiousness later earned him the nickname 'Rasputin', which means 'the debauched one'. At eighteen he underwent a religious conversion and joined a monastery at Verkhoture, where he was introduced to the Khlysty flagellants. Perhaps perverting their beliefs, he preached that the way to get closest to God was to achieve 'holy powerlessness' through sexual exhaustion. The ritual of 'rejoicing' – sexual orgies – brought him many followers.

Rather than become a monk, Rasputin returned home, married and fathered four children – but he could not settle down. He travelled to Mount Athos in Greece and Jerusalem, and then wandered around Russia as a self-proclaimed holy man.

By the time he reached St Petersburg in 1903, Rasputin had a powerful reputation as a mystic, a healer and a clairvoyant. In 1905 he was introduced at court. Tsar Nicholas's son Alexis was a haemophiliac and Rasputin was called on to tend to the young tsarevich. It was found that he could somehow successfully ease the child's condition – perhaps through hypnosis.

'God has seen your tears and heard your prayers,' Rasputin told the Tsarina, his mother. 'Fear not, the child will not die.'

Rasputin also gave practical advice about Alexis's care,

halting the use of leeches (with their anticoagulant saliva) to 'bleed' the child. He stopped Alexis' administration with aspirin (which was then thought to be a wonder drug, but which would have only worsened the young boy's haemophilia). He kept Alexis away from doctors and recommended rest, which he said would allow the natural healing processes to work.

While Rasputin remained a paragon of chastity and humility in court, outside he continued to indulge himself in scandalous ways. In 1911 the prime minister drew up a long bill of Rasputin's offences and the Tsar expelled him from court, but he was soon recalled by the Tsarina, who feared for her son's life. When Tsar Nicholas was called to the front line during the First World War and the Tsarina was left in charge, Rasputin began to meddle in government affairs. He and the Tsarina were so close that there were rumours that they were lovers.

An attempt was made on his life on 29 June 1914 when Khioniya Guseva, former prostitute and one-time follower of Rasputin, stabbed him in the belly when he was visiting his wife and children.

'I have killed the Antichrist,' she cried.

Although she ruptured his stomach wall and part of his intestine protruded, Rasputin recovered after surgery, although he continued to take opium for pain relief thereafter.

On 30 December 1916, a gang of conservative noblemen fed him poisoned cake and wine. When he fell into a coma, Prince Felix Yusupov, a homosexual who was said to have been rebuffed by Rasputin several times, shot him four times. A second assassin pulled out a knife and castrated Rasputin, throwing his severed penis across the room. Rasputin was then tied up and thrown in the icy Neva River, where he finally drowned and died.

30

THE ASSASSINS

The Murderous Order of Islam

On a thirteen-year journey through the Middle East, the Spanish rabbi Benjamin of Tudela visited Syria in AD 1167, which he described as a place inhabited by a war-like sect hidden in remote mountain fortresses and commanded by a mysterious leader known as the Old Man of the Mountain. Over the next two centuries, crusaders and other travellers brought back their own stories of the Assassins, a sect trained from childhood to murder at the whim of their leader. High on intoxicating drugs, their recruits were kept in paradisiacal gardens and given fine food and beautiful women. They became the most famous killer cult in history.

The Order of the Assassins was founded by Hassan-i Sabbah in twelfth-century Daylam in Iran. He was the leader of the Nizari Ismailis, a breakaway group from the Ismaili branch of Shia Islam which existed from the eleventh to the thirteenth century. In its early years, it considered murdering its enemies to be a religious duty.

The Arabic word for assassin, *hashish*, means a 'hashish smoker', and refers to the Assassins' alleged practice of taking hashish to induce ecstatic visions of paradise before setting out to face martyrdom. The historical existence of this practice, however, is doubtful. The stories told by Marco Polo and other travellers about hedonistic, drugged devotees, who were given a foretaste of eternal bliss before death, are not confirmed by any known Ismaili source. Nor did they inhabit gardens or were given fine food and beautiful women; in reality, their dusty mountain forts were often besieged and the presence of women was prohibited during military campaigns.

In 1090 Hassan-i Sabbah, along with some Persian allies, seized the hill fortress of Alamut in Daylam. Opposing the growing empire of the Seljuq Turks, he had established a loose but cohesive state, which he defended by sending assassins into enemy camps and cities to murder the generals and statesmen who opposed him. Unable to confront the superior Seljuq armies on the battlefield, instead, the Nizaris sent devotees to infiltrate the households of enemy leaders and kill them. Murders were often carried out publicly in broad daylight for maximum effect.

With Hassan-i Sabbah as Grand Master, the Order of the Assassins was given a hierarchical structure. Under Sabbah were the Greater Propagandists, followed by the regular Propagandists, the Companions and the Adherents, the latter two groups comprising those who were trained to become the killers called Fida'is ('self-sacrificing agents'). They were young and fit, but also cold and calculating. They were generally intelligent and well-read because they needed to know the language and culture of their enemies. They were also trained in deceit, stealth and disguise, and given religious instruction before being sent out on suicide missions.

Their first victim was the Seljuq sultan Nizam al-Mulk, who was assassinated on his way from Isfahan to Baghdad. A killer disguised as a dervish – a Sufi Muslim – stabbed him.

Other terror tactics were used. When the next Sultan of the Seljuq, Ahmad Sanjar, rebuffed some Assassin ambassadors, he woke one morning to find a dagger stuck in the ground beside his bed. A message from Sabbah arrived afterwards, wishing that 'the dagger which was struck in the hard ground' had been instead 'planted on [the sultan's] soft breast'.

For the next several decades, in a bid to appease the Nizaris, the Seljuq maintained a ceasefire with them. Sultan Ahmed Sanjar even provided pensions for the Assassins from the taxes he was owed by them, gave them grants and licences, and allowed them to collect their own tolls from travellers.

In the twelfth century the Nizari extended their activities into Syria, seizing a group of castles in the Al-Ansariyah Mountains. They were led by the legendary Rashid ad-Din as-Sinan, who was the leader of the Syrian branch of the Assassins and operated independently of the headquarters of the cult in Alamut. He made several attempts on the life of the Ayyubid leader, Saladin, a Sunni Kurd, who opposed the Ismaili Shia sect. Rashid, like Sabbah, was given the soubriquet 'shaykh al-jabal'. This was in fact the Arabic for 'mountain chief', but it was mistranslated as the 'old man of the mountain' and so the legendary name for the leader of the Assassins lived on.

The story goes that Count Henry of Champagne visited Grand Master Rashid ad-Din Sinan at al-Kahf at his castle in Syria on his return from Armenia. The count claimed to have the most powerful army in the world and he boasted that, at any moment, he could defeat the Assassins because his army was ten times larger than that of the Grand Master. Rashid replied that his army was, in fact, the most powerful of all and, to prove it, he ordered one of his men to jump from the top of his castle. The man did so and fell to his death. The count immediately acknowledged that Rashid's army must be the strongest because his men would do anything he commanded.

Over 300 years the Assassins killed two caliphs, along with many viziers, sultans and crusaders. The Assassins selected their victims strategically, eliminating those who posed the greatest threat to Ismaili Shias, particularly those who had committed massacres.

Assassin power came to an end when the Mongols invaded Persia. One by one their castles fell, until, in 1256, the headquarters of the cult at Alamut was overrun. Their Syrian fortresses were gradually subjugated by the Mamluk sultan, Baybars I, and the Mamluk governors employed the remaining Assassins as paid killers. Nizaris were also used as mercenaries by the kings of Hungary before they were expelled from the country by the Inquisition.

The influence of the Nizaris continued to wane, but followers are still found in Iran, Persia and Central Asia. The largest group is to be found in India and Pakistan. They are known as Khojas, a caste of people who converted from Hinduism in the fourteenth century and are followers of the Aga Khan, the leader of the now peaceable Nizari sect of Ismali Muslims.

THE SECRET GARDEN OF PARADISE

In Marco Polo's account of the Assassins, he described the 'secret garden of paradise' where they were taken as recruits. He wrote:

The Old Man was called in their language Aloadin. He had caused a certain valley between two mountains to be enclosed, and had turned it into a garden, the largest and most beautiful that ever was seen, filled with every variety of fruit. In it were erected pavilions and palaces the most elegant that can be imagined, all covered with gilding and exquisite painting. And there were runnels too, flowing freely with wine and milk and honey and water; and numbers of ladies and of the most beautiful maidens in the world, who could play on all manner of instruments, and sung most sweetly and danced in a manner that it was charming to behold. For the Old Man desired to make his people believe that this was actually Paradise. So he had fashioned it after the description that Muhummad gave of his paradise, to wit, that it should be a beautiful garden running with conduits of wine and milk and honey and water, and full of lovely women for the delectation of all its inmates.

'Now no man was allowed to enter the garden save those whom he intended to be his Assassins. There was a fortress at the entrance to the garden, strong enough to resist all the world, and there was no other way to get in. He kept at his court a number of the youths of the country, from twelve to twenty years of age, such as had a taste for soldiering, and to these he used to tell tales about Paradise, just as Muhammad had been wont to do, and they believed in him just as the Saracens believed Muhammad. Then he would introduce them into his garden, some four, or six, or ten at a time, having first made them drink a certain potion which cast them into a deep sleep, and then causing them to be lifted and carried in. So when they awoke, they found themselves in the garden.'

31

CHILDREN OF GOD

Freaking Out for Jesus

The late 1960s and early 1970s was a time when everybody was seen to be freaking out. Usually this involved the obvious: a loud rock music scene and the consumption of hallucinogenic drugs. On the fringes, some charismatic evangelical Christian preachers realized that they could manipulate young people to freak out about Jesus as well. One of the most effective of these preachers was David Berg. A former Methodist minister, by the late 1960s he was middle-aged, pot-bellied and balding. For some years, he had been dragging his family around the Midwest, preaching the gospel of the Lord to no effect, but in 1968 he turned up in California when the hippie movement was in full swing. He saw an opportunity.

The generation of drop-outs that congregated along the beaches of California were attracted to the club Berg established, which he called Teens for Christ. There they heard the homespun philosophy of the self-styled 'Moses' or 'Father' David, who delivered traditional evangelical teachings dressed up in the language of sex, drugs and rock 'n' roll. Berg's wife, Jane, otherwise known as 'Mother', dished out peanut-butter sandwiches. Many of Berg's young recruits had already abandoned their families, jobs and the other trappings of 'straight' life. They were attracted by Berg's anti-establishment view of the meaning of life and the free food, as well.

It was a journalist who dubbed Berg's followers the 'Children of God' – or, more pejoratively, 'Jesus Freaks'. Berg seized on the title. He became a tele-evangelist, appealing particularly to the young. And when Jeremy Spencer, the guitarist of the famous rock band Fleetwood Mac, quit mid-tour and joined the Children of God, the movement acquired a new cachet.

Initially Berg preached the joys of celibacy, but when an attractive new young female recruit named Karen Zerby (she was rechristened as 'Maria') joined the cult, Berg began to proclaim the joys of free love. He declared that Maria was his second wife, though his first wife, Jane, stayed with the cult. He also 'shared' the wives of other cult members.

Berg preached that, since God was love, anything went sexually – including incest and paedophilia. However, when allegations of the sexual abuse suffered by children in the cult surfaced in the press, Berg back-pedalled on his stance on paedophilia, declaring it an excommunicable offence. Homosexuality was later banned as well, with Berg citing Biblical injunctions against it.

Recruits had to give up everything they owned to the cult. They were warned of the forthcoming apocalypse and that, if they left, they should give up any hope of salvation.

Children of God (COG) were expected to cut all ties with their families and friends outside the cult. However, in 1972, an organization called FREECOG was set up to help parents to reclaim their children from the cult. It was the first of the modern anti-cult organizations whose aim was to kidnap cult members and subject them to intensive anti-brainwashing techniques. The Children of God was also under investigation by the American authorities, so Berg decamped to England and set up his new headquarters in the south-east, in Bromley.

The popularity of the cult spread widely throughout the world, but Berg feared that it was getting beyond his control. Sect leaders in various countries were taking too much authority upon themselves, he thought, and so in 1978 he dismissed over 300 of them – including his own daughter and her husband, who were COG leaders in South America. He also sacked 2,600 members, which was a third of the membership at the time. Those who remained were invited to join Berg's new brainchild, the Family of Love, which, chillingly, began calling itself the 'Family'.

To boost their membership numbers, Berg introduced 'flirty fishing'. The idea to encourage this form of evangelistic religious prostitution originated from his second wife, Maria, who had been taking other men to bed and successfully converting them for years. Christ was a fisher of men and, according to Berg, in order to fish, you need bait. To this end, he sent out young, attractive female cult members – both single and married – to pick up men in bars and clubs. Once bedded, these men would be lured into the fold. In the 1980s, however, the fear of AIDS put a stop to flirty fishing. It is not known how effective a recruiting method it was, although some say it did, in fact, bring more women into the cult.

Since then, sexual freedom has been confined to cult members only and this freedom is not extended to new recruits until they have completed a six-month probationary period. Members of the Children of God live a communal life, supported by donations and sales of their posters, music cassettes and videos. Sometimes cult members take ordinary jobs if more income is needed for the cult.

By and large, Children of God does not look after its members well. Police inquiries established that of 1,000 members recruited in the south of England during the 1980s, at least 116 died over a ten-year period. When prosecutions of the Children of God began in 1994, Berg mysteriously disappeared. The cult said he had suddenly died, but others believed he went into hiding in Europe. Berg's second wife, Maria – a.k.a Mama Maria, Queen Maria, Maria David and Maria Fontaine – took over.

In November 1995, Lord Justice Ward declared that Berg

was sexually depraved and that the rights of children in the cult had been violated. Despite this, he ruled that a 28-year-old cult member could keep her three-year-old son – despite the protests of the child's grandmother – provided that she renounced the teachings of David Berg. The cult's spokeswoman proclaimed that the verdict was a vindication.

Some of the cult's more abusive practices were outlawed by the Love Charter, introduced in February 1995. This remained in force when the Family became the 'Family International' in 2004. Its members became soldiers in the spiritual war of good versus evil for the souls and hearts of men. Maria apparently 'revealed' the presence of the biblical 'keys to the kingdom [of God]' which had lain hidden and unused for centuries. This did not mean that the cult had lost its sexual dimension, however. Members were encouraged to imagine they were being joined by Jesus during intercourse and masturbation – though during this ecstatic fantasy men were required to visualize themselves as women, in order to avoid any hint of homosexuality.

THE JESUS ARMY

Another group of Jesus Freaks that took root in Britain were members of the so-called 'Jesus Army'. This group had its beginnings in 1969, when Baptist minister Noel Stanton and some members of his chapel in Northampton started speaking in tongues. They began preaching the gospel there in the new hippie jargon of the 'Jesus Revolution'.

Soon the church became too small for its growing congregation. Stanton raised donations and bought buildings to house his followers, and his congregation became a community, supported by the produce of its New Creation Farm.

These communal houses spread across the UK. The Jesus Army also owned health-food shops, builders, plumbers and a clothes store. Members were ferried around in brightly painted 'Battle buses' and wore camouflage jackets, combat gear and army boots.

Its philosophy was that of straightforward, evangelical Christianity, but Stanton preached with theatrical display. He condemned sports, drinking and 'worldly music', and he took a hammer to guitars, videos and music cassettes.

In the communal houses, everything was shared, including money and clothes. Watching TV and listening to the radio were banned, as were most newspapers. Only religious music was played. The Jesus Army did not celebrate Christian festivals such as Christmas on the grounds that they had their origins in paganism. Sex was actively discouraged. Even long-married couples were required to sleep in separate beds. Romantic liaisons between members required the permission of the leadership, and traditional gender roles were strictly enforced.

Recruits were required to hand over everything they owned to the army. But this was not the rip-off tactic used by other cults in order to prevent members' defection, leaving those who contemplated leaving to face a life of poverty, the cult claimed. The Jesus Army (now known as the Jesus Fellowship) says that it keeps its members' money in a separate trust fund, which is returned to them, sometimes with interest, if they decided to leave the church.

Noel Stanton died in 2009, eight years before allegations of sexual, physical and financial abuse were laid at his door.

32

NUWAUBIAN NATION

The Indigenous People of These Shores

The United Nuwaubian Nation of Moors is an American black separatist movement. Its leader, Dwight 'Malachi' York, claimed: 'We are the Indigenous people of these shores, before the settlers from Europe came to these shores spreading their way of life, their filth and religion.' According to the *Intelligence Report* of the Southern Poverty Law Center, a periodical that monitors the radical right in the US, Nuwaubianism 'mixes black supremacist ideas with worship of the Egyptians and their pyramids, a belief in UFOs and various conspiracies related to the Illuminati and the Bilderbergers'.

Born in 1945, Dwight York was arrested for statutory rape in 1964 after having sex with a thirteen-year-old girl. He was given a suspended sentence and put on probation. Later that year he was arrested for assault, possession of a deadly weapon and resisting arrest, and he subsequently served three years in prison.

Upon his release he started to work as a street pedlar in Harlem, selling incense and pamphlets about race he had written. He picked up a handful of followers and moved some of them into the apartment where he lived with his wife. He called his small following Ansar Pure Sufi, in keeping with the black nationalists' embrace of Islam.

In the early 1970s the sect moved to Brooklyn, where they

became known as the Ansaru Allah Community. They supported themselves by selling pamphlets, and people were encouraged to come and hear the preaching of the self-styled Dr Malachi Z. York. Soon the Ansaru Allah Community ran bookshops, gift shops, clothes shops and grocery shops. Branches of the church opened in Trinidad, London and Toronto.

Five hundred Ansaru Allah Community members lived in twenty barrack-style apartments in the Bushwick district of Brooklyn. In order to join the cult they were required by York to surrender their possessions and work for free. Those who did not succeed in selling their quota of pamphlets were beaten up. Members had to ask permission to have sex, even with their spouses, and York used female members – some of whom were underage – as his personal harem.

As its popularity increased, the Ansaru Allah Community had enough money to move to a mansion in the Catskills worth five million dollars. It was here that York molested girls as young as six and had sex with twelve-year-olds.

The group began to produce books, often plagiarizing other New Age works. They mixed together UFOs, the religion of ancient Egypt, the myth of Atlantis and Bible stories; and from the Nation of Islam, York borrowed the idea that white people were 'devils' whose light skin was the result of leprosy and having sex with dogs.

In 1993 the cult moved to a remote 476-acre estate in Putnam County, Georgia. This may have been prompted by an FBI investigation into offences allegedly committed by members, including arson, welfare fraud and the illegal possession of weapons. In Georgia, York dropped the pretence of being a Muslim and claimed he was a Native American, dubbing himself the 'Chief Black Eagle' of the 'Yamassee Tribe of Native Americans'. He also claimed to be, at once, a god from outer space, a member of the Sudanese royal family and a descendent of the Olmec people of Mesoamerica – polygamy and underage sex were part of their culture, apparently. June marked an annual celebration of a 'Saviour's Day' in York's name. Members had to pay twenty-five dollars for a Nuwaubian passport to allow them to enter or leave the compound and get past the armed guards.

Adopting an Ancient Egyptian motif, the cult then became known as the 'United Nuwaubian Nation of Moors'. York named their new compound Tama-Re and commanded his followers to build two wood-and-plaster pyramids. To earn more money, he set up a nightclub called Club Ramses in one of the pyramids. When the police closed it down for violating zoning regulations, the county sheriff received death threats, the attorney representing the county against the Nuwaubians was harassed and the county government disrupted. The enforced closure of the club was said by some to be racist, and Al Sharpton and Jesse Jackson came to lend their support to York.

Malachi York's oldest son, Jacob, who had left the cult in 1990, confronted his father, who shamelessly retorted: 'I don't believe in any of this shit. If I had to dress up like a nun, if I had to be a Jew, I'd do it for this type of money.'

Jacob York went on to help the authorities with their investigation into abuses going on inside the cult. The authorities had realized something was wrong when a number of underage Nuwaubian girls had given birth in local hospitals. Fearing a Waco-style shoot-out, the FBI waited until York Senior left the compound before arresting him and his favourite wife. Then, on 8 May 2002, 300 agents raided the compound, where they met no resistance. They confiscated thirty guns.

York was indicted on 120 counts, including 74 counts of child molestation, 29 counts of aggravated child molestation, and one count of rape. Five charges of racketeering and six of transporting children across state lines for the purpose of sexual intercourse followed.

Accepting a plea bargain (a shortened jail term because York had agreed to plead guilty), York faced just fifteen years in jail.

But a federal judge threw this out, and York got 135 years. The federal government seized Tama-Re and York's assets and evicted his followers. Many kept the faith, though. Two hundred turned up to demonstrate in September 2005 in Atlanta, where York's appeal against his sentence was rejected.

In August 2009, 300 followers turned up at the federal courthouse in Macon in Georgia, to support a further appeal. People involved in the case were harassed and followers continue to make attempts to get York out of jail.

The *Atlanta Journal-Constitution* reported that, in 2014, authorities found Nuwaubian Nation literature and notes in the home of a man who was charged with starving his baby to death. In a feature from 2015, the news website Vice reported that a bookshop in Brooklyn called 'All Eyes on Egipt' [sic] still sold York's works, along with those of other conspiracy theorists. Local news website Patch.com reported the presence of the Nuwaubian Nation in Hartford, Connecticut, and an investigation by *People* magazine found that the cult still existed in 2018.

Meanwhile, the US Supreme Court refused to hear York's latest appeal. Dwight York is held in ADX Florence, a maximum-security federal prison in Florence, Colorado, and he won't be eligible for parole until 2122.

THE SAYINGS OF DWIGHT YORK

'White people are the devil. They say the Nuwaubians are not racist – bullcrap! I am ... White people are devils – always was, always will be.'

From the lecture 'Egipt [sic] and the Mask of God'

'The Nuwbuns [sic] were the dark brown-to-black-skin, woolly-hair original Egyptians ... the Black race's greatness has been accepted In America and many books as people of Timbuktu Africa or the Olmecians from Uganda, Africa, who migrated and walked here to North and South America to set up colonies way before the continental drift.'

Proclamation in Augusta, Georgia, 2001

'Christianity is merely a tool used by the Devil (Paleman) to keep you, the Nubian (Black) man, woman, and child blind to your true heritage and perfect way of life (Islam). It is another means of slavery.'

From an undated essay 'Santa or Satan? The Fallacy of Christmas'

'The Caucasian has not been chosen to lead the world. They lack true emotions in their creation. We never intended them to be peaceful. They were bred to be killers, with low reproduction levels and a short life span. What you call Negroid was to live thousand years each and the other humans 120 years. But the warrior seed of Caucasians is only sixty years old. They were only created to fight other invading races, to protect the God race Negroids. But they went insane, lost control when they were left unattended. They were never to taste blood. They did, and their true nature came out ... Because their reproduction levels were cut short, their sexual organs were made the smallest so that the female of their race will want to breed with Negroids to breed themselves out of existence after six thousand years. It took six hundred years to breed them, part man and part beast.'

From a letter dated 10 November 2004

33

SWEDENBORGIANISM

The New Church

On Easter Monday in 1744, the scientist and inventor Emanuel Swedenborg had a vision. It was the first of a series of visions, during which he visited heaven and hell to converse with angels, demons and other spirits and which culminated in a 'spiritual awakening'. This prompted him to give up his scientific work and devote himself to religion. He went on to write eighteen theological works. The result was a new religious movement and the establishment of the New Church in England in 1787, although his writing was considered heretical in his native Sweden and banned. Several branches of the New Church still exist in the UK, US, Canada and the Netherlands.

Born in Stockholm in 1688, Emanuel Swedenborg was the son of a distinguished professor of theology at Uppsala University, one Jesper Swedberg, who was ennobled as Swedenborg after being appointed Bishop of Skara. Jesper Swedberg translated the Bible into Swedish and held the unconventional belief that angels and spirits were present in everyday life – views that greatly influenced his son.

Emanuel left Sweden to continue his education at the age of twenty-two and spent four years in London studying physics, mechanics and philosophy. Upon returning home in 1715, he became the assessor for the Swedish Board of Mines and published a scientific periodical entitled *Daedalus Hyperboreus* (*The Northern Daedalus*) which was a record of various mechanical and mathematical inventions and discoveries, and which included his own plans for a flying machine.

In the 1730s his interests turned to the study of anatomy and physiology, and he became increasingly interested in spiritual matters. He published the three-volume *Opera philosophica et mineralis* (*Philosophical and Mineralogical Works*) in 1735, in which he attempted to combine a philosophical ideas with metallurgy. The chapters on the smelting of iron and copper earned him an international reputation. That same year he also published *De Infinito* (*On the Infinite*) in which he tried to explain how the body was connected to the soul.

In 1743 he travelled abroad to work on *Regnum animale* (*The Animal Kingdom*) and began to record his dreams, some erotic, some visionary and some disturbing. After his vision in 1744 he began work on *De cultu et amore Dei* (*The Worship and Love of God*), which was published in London in 1745. It was there that he had the vision that he felt had given him access to heaven and hell. He left his job at the Board of Mines and began his spiritual reinterpretation of the Bible, which was published under the title *Arcana Caelestia* (*The Heavenly Arcana*, or as *Heavenly Mysteries* or *Secrets of Heaven* in its various English-language editions). The first volume began:

> From the mere letter of the Word of the Old Testament no one would ever discern the fact that this part of the Word contains deep secrets of heaven, and that everything within it both in general and in particular bears reference to the Lord, to His heaven, to the church, to religious belief, and to all things connected therewith; for from the letter or sense of the letter all that anyone can see is that – to speak generally – everything therein has reference merely to the external rites and ordinances of the Jewish Church. Yet the truth is

that everywhere in that Word there are internal things which never appear at all in the external things except a very few which the Lord revealed and explained to the Apostles; such as that the sacrifices signify the Lord; that the land of Canaan and Jerusalem signify heaven – on which account they are called the Heavenly Canaan and Jerusalem – and that Paradise has a similar signification.

There were eight volumes of this, and another fourteen works of a spiritual nature were published in his lifetime. In *The Heavenly Doctrine*, published in 1758, he claimed the Last Judgement had taken place the previous year, but that it had happened in the spiritual realm and he had witnessed it. The Second Coming of Christ had also taken place – not by Jesus visiting the world in person, but through Swedenborg's own revelation of the inner, spiritual sense of the Word. Swedenborg's credo, *Vera Christiana Religio* (*The True Christian Religion*) was his last published work, in Amsterdam, in 1771.

In 1768, while Swedenborg was abroad, a trial for heresy against him and his works had already begun in Sweden. His writings were banned there in 1770. He died in 1772, but, fifteen years later, his New Church movement began to take root in England. Several churches sprang up, and the first General Conference of the New Church was held in London in 1789. In America, the first General Convention of the New Church, also known as the Swedenborgian Church of North America, was held in 1817.

With the growth of theosophy and occultism in the nineteenth century, Swedenborg's accounts of his visits to heaven and hell became of particular interest to many. However, membership of the New Church remained small and the movement is now thought to have fewer than 10,000 followers worldwide.

Notable adherents have included the poets William Blake and Robert Frost and the advocate for the deaf-blind, Helen Keller. Swedenborg is also thought to have influenced Joseph Smith, the founder of Mormonism, and Carl Jung, the founder of analytical psychology. Jung was particularly interested in the reported incidents of Swedenborg's clairvoyance. On 19 July 1759, a fire had broken out in Stockholm, destroying some 300 houses and making 2,000 people homeless. Swedenborg was 250 miles away at the time, but he told friends about the fire at dinner that evening, despite the fact that it would have taken a messenger two or three days to bring that news from Stockholm which later confirmed Swedenborg's account in detail.

At another dinner, Swedenborg told a cloth manufacturer: 'You had better go to your mills, sir.' The man went and found that a large piece of cloth had fallen down near the furnace and had caught fire. If he had delayed a moment longer, his whole factory would have been ablaze. Then, when in 1758 Swedenborg visited Queen Louisa Ulrika of Sweden, who had asked him to tell her something about her dead brother Prince Augustus William of Prussia, Swedenborg whispered a reply into her ear. The queen turned pale. She explained that what he had told her was something only she and her brother could have known.

SWEDENBORG'S VISION

In April 1745 Emanuel Swedenborg was in London. One afternoon, he was having a late lunch in a private room at an inn. Towards the end of the meal he noticed a sort of dimness before his eyes. It grew darker, and then he saw the floor covered with horrible crawling creatures such as snakes and frogs. This is Swedenborg's account.

> I was astounded, for I was in full possession of my senses and had clear thoughts. At last the darkness prevailed, and then suddenly it dispersed and I saw a man sitting in a corner of the room. As I was then quite alone, I became

very much frightened at his speech, for he said, 'Eat not so much!'

Again all became black before my eyes, but immediately it cleared away and I found myself alone in the room. Such an unexpected terror hastened my return to my room. I showed no concern before the landlord but considered well what had happened and could not look upon it as a matter of chance or produced by a physical cause.

I went to my room, but that night the same man revealed himself to me again. I was not frightened then. He said that he was the Lord God, the Creator and Redeemer of the world and that He had chosen me to declare to men the spiritual contents of Scripture; and that He Himself would declare to me what I should write on this subject.

Then, on that same night, the world of spirits, hell and heaven were opened to me with full conviction. I recognized there many acquaintances of every condition in life. And from that day on I gave up all practice of worldly letters and devoted my labour to spiritual things.

34

THE FUNDAMENTALIST CHURCH OF JESUS CHRIST OF LATTER-DAY SAINTS

The Council of God

As you may remember from Chapter 25, in 1887 the US Congress passed the Edmunds–Tucker Act, which removed the legal status of the Church of Jesus Christ of Latter-Day Saints and authorized the federal government to seize its assets. Three years later, the Supreme Court upheld this and disenfranchized those members of the church who practised polygamy or believed that plural marriage was constitutional. Prominent Mormon polygamists were arrested. Soon after, the president of the church, Wilford Woodruff, had a revelation, apparently from Jesus Christ, who had decreed that plural marriage should end. A manifesto to that effect was published, but some fundamentalist followers refused to give up the polygamy and broke away to form their own church.

Many members living around Short Creek, Utah, continued the practice of polygamy, but soon ran into problems with the law once again. As Utah had not previously been recognized as a state but only a territory, those fundamentalist followers had been able to continue living there to ignore federal law. After multiple applications, Utah (with its 60 per cent Mormon population) was granted statehood in 1896 – but only provided it outlawed polygamy. This put the Church of Jesus Christ of Latter-Day Saints under immense pressure, and so it issued a second manifesto in 1904 which stated that anyone who entered into a polygamous marriage would be excommunicated. But those still committed to the practice continued to congregate at Short Creek.

In 1913 Short Creek was split into the twin cities of Hildale in Utah and Colorado in Arizona. A year earlier Lorin C. Woolley, a Mormon from Centennial Park in Arizona, had published a statement which he attributed to Woodruff's predecessor, John Taylor. It concerned a revelation which John Taylor had apparently received in 1886, which had then led to the church's founder, Joseph Smith, confirming that 'celestial' or plural marriage should be the rule from henceforth. This new 'truth' gave the polygamous inhabitants of Utah the conviction to continue practising polygamy and to flee across the state border to Arizona, still a territory until 1912, when raided by the police.

Woolley, his father and three others – plus the long-dead Joseph Smith and John Taylor, whose 'spiritual' participation they quoted to give their group legitimacy – formed the 'Council of Friends', a new sect that claimed apostolic authority over the Church of Jesus Christ of Latter-Day Saints, which had excommunicated Woolley in 1924. More members joined them between 1929 and 1933. In 1935 the Church of Jesus Christ of Latter-Day Saints excommunicated the remaining residents of Short Creek who refused to sign an oath renouncing polygamy. Many of these cast-out members went on to join the Council of Friends.

By the time of Woolley's death in 1934, a number of splinter groups had formed within the Council of God, reacting against Woolley's successor, John Y. Barlow, and his claim to be a prophet called upon by God to lead. Barlow himself was succeeded by Joseph White Musser, who was the leader of the new sect when the Arizona authorities cracked down on them. At dawn on 26 July 1953, the Arizona National Guard entered Short Creek. The residents had received a tip-off and quickly assembled themselves so that they would be found innocently singing hymns in the school-house, rather than in their houses, clearly living in polygamous families. The authorities were not deceived by their ruse, and arrested and charged them with insurrection. Many of the children were not returned to their parents for two years – some not at all.

The raid, however, was counterproductive. The American public had been against polygamy, but they saw a heavy-handed raid on otherwise innocent people as un-American. 'By what stretch of the imagination could the actions of the Short Creek children be classified as insurrection?' asked the *Arizona Republic*. Governor John Howard Pyle, who had authorized the raid, wasn't voted in again at the next election. Even mainstream Mormons, who were keen to distance themselves from the polygamous members of the Council of God, openly condemned the removal of children from their parents.

The Council of God community at Short Creek recovered and formally established the new Fundamentalist Church of Jesus Christ of Latter-Day Saints in 1991. In 2003 members of the Fundamentalist Church sought refuge in Texas, where they established the Yearning for Zion Ranch, on a 1,700-acre site outside Eldorado. Five hundred Fundamentalist Church followers relocated there. Their president, Warren Jeffs, attended the dedication ceremony at the ranch in 2005 before returning to Arizona, where he reportedly performed marriage ceremonies involving underage girls and older men.

In 2006 Jeffs was charged with child sexual abuse in Arizona and with being an accomplice to statutory rape in Utah. He was put on the FBI's 'Ten Most Wanted Fugitives' list, with a 100,000-dollar reward on his head. His nephew, Brent W. Jeffs, was also seeking damages against him, alleging that his uncle had repeatedly sodomized him when he was five. Two of his brothers had suffered the same abuse, he said, and one had subsequently killed himself. Warren Jeffs was arrested in Nevada and returned to Utah to stand trial.

The following year Jeffs stood down as president of the Fundamentalist Church. He was found guilty on two counts of being an accomplice to rape and was sentenced to ten years in jail. In 2010, however, the Utah Supreme Court overturned the verdict, citing deficient jury instructions. Jeffs was then sent to Arizona, where he faced charges of sexual abuse. When proceedings there stalled, he was sent to Texas, where he was finally convicted of the sexual assault of two girls – one aged twelve, the other fifteen – whom he had taken as polygamous wives, and he was given the maximum sentence: life, plus twenty years.

In 2008 the Yearning for Zion Ranch was raided and 439 children were removed from the premises. Twelve men were charged with offences connected with underage marriages; six were convicted. Later on, the State of Texas seized the ranch on the grounds that it had been used for the systematic sexual abuse of children. Meanwhile, in Arizona, the Colorado city/Hildale marshal's office was disbanded, as it was judged to have been too close to the Fundamentalist Church of Jesus Christ of Latter-Day Saints and acted as its de facto law enforcement arm.

The Fundamentalist Church has also been accused of racism. This is their credo, according to Warren Jeffs:

The black race is the people through which the devil has always been able to bring evil unto the earth. [Cain was] cursed with a black skin and he is the father of the Negro people. He has great power, can appear and disappear. He is used by the devil, as a mortal man, to do great evils.

Today you can see a black man with a white woman, et cetera. A great evil has happened on this land because the devil knows that if all the people have Negro blood, there will be nobody worthy to have the priesthood ... If you marry a person who has connections with a Negro, you would become cursed.

They also consider homosexuality to be a heinous crime. In Jeffs' words, 'The people grew so evil, the men started to marry the men and the women married the women. This is the worst evil act you can do, next to murder. It is like murder. Whenever people commit that sin, then the Lord destroys them.'

Jeffs has also alluded to his belief that serious sins, apparently including apostasy, can only be atoned for by the death of the sinner. He had said this too: 'I want to remind you what the prophets have taught us, that whenever a man of God is commanded to kill another man, he is never bloodthirsty.' Truly, a dangerous creed.

PLACEMENT MARRIAGE

Under the leadership of Warren Jeffs, the wives of male members of the church who had been excommunicated were reassigned to other male followers.

'You can't go to heaven and be a god unless you have more than one wife,' he said.

He also assigned underage girls to men many years their senior, sometimes incestuously. This led to a high incidence of children with birth defects being born in the cult.

Charlene Jeffs, the estranged wife of Warren's brother, Lyle, has reported that women were only allowed to have sex with designated 'seed bearers'. The woman's husband was supposed to hold the woman's hand while the seed bearer attempted to impregnate her. During a battle for custody of two of her children, Charlene also described the 'Law of Sarah', which decreed that women in the cult should perform sex acts on one another, supposedly to prepare them for a sexual encounter with a man high up in the church's leadership.

According to Lorin Holm, who claimed to have been part of Warren Jeffs' 'inner circle' before he was excommunicated from the Fundamentalist Church in 2011, the Law of Sarah, as practised at the Yearning for Zion Ranch, was akin to a sex show, with Jeffs participating and sermonizing throughout. Mothers who would not take part in the enactment of the Law of Sarah were sent away to 'redeem themselves', and their children were given to other women.

One of the consequences of men marrying multiple women in their community was that there were not enough of them to go around for all the men to have more than one wife. To reduce the competition for wives, boys – usually between the ages of thirteen and twenty-one – were expelled from the sect for very minor offences, such as talking to a girl, playing football or watching television.

'I have been instructed that any young man who will not leave our girls alone is to be sent away and not allowed to be among us, even before they destroy the girl,' Warren Jeffs had said.

These so-called 'lost boys' – young men who were expelled from the Fundamentalist Church – had received little education beyond Bible study and been brought up with the idea that life outside the cult was evil. Girls who refused to be part of a polygamous marriage were also pressured to leave and were similarly ill-equipped for life outside the cult.

35

RAËLISM

Humankind Made By Extraterrestrials

In 1973 twenty-seven-year-old former pop singer and motor-sports journalist Claude Vorilhon was driving in central France. Fancying some fresh air, he parked his car and took a stroll around the craters of a nearby extinct volcano called Puy-de-Lassolas. There, he said, he saw a UFO land and a small French-speaking alien get out. Over the course of several meetings, the alien explained that scientists from its planet had used the earth as a laboratory to create life. Vorilhon, the alien said, had been picked to explain this to the people of the world. He was to change his name to 'Raël' – which meant 'messenger' – and was to be their ambassador on earth.

Born in Vichy in 1946, Claude Vorilhon ran away from boarding school at the age of fifteen and hitchhiked to Paris, where he found himself living on the streets. To make money, he started singing in cabarets and making records, although his ambition was to be a racing driver. But when he started his own magazine, *Autopop*, manufacturers would lend him sports cars to test-drive on the racing circuit.

He had been doing this for three years when he had his encounter with the alien. The alien apparently said he was an 'Elohim', which he explained means 'Those who came from the sky' and has been mistranslated as 'God' in the Bible. They met for six consecutive days so that the alien could dictate the content of the book Raël would eventually publish as *The Book Which Tells the Truth*. Between sessions, Raël said, he received the devoted attentions of six 'voluptuous and bewitching' female robots.

To promote the book, Raël left journalism, appeared on television and gave public talks. He then founded MADECH, which stood for the 'Mouvement pour l'Accueil Des Elohim, Créateurs de l'Humanité' (Movement for Welcoming the Elohim, Creators of Humanity), as well as 'Moise À Devancé Elie et le Christ' (Moses Preceded Elijah and the Christ [sic], although the initial letters of this sentence only create the word MADEC, spelling not being Vorilhon's strongest suit). This became the International Raëlian Movement.

In 1975 Raël said he was taken to the Elohim's home planet, where he met Buddha, Moses, Jesus and Muhammad. There he was shown the factory where biological robots were made and heard about the need for 'geniocracy': government by those who are clever and compassionate.

The Raëlian Movement spread worldwide, soon claiming a following of some 90,000 members. Vorilhon moved the headquarters to Canada, where UFOland was established as the first embassy for extra-terrestrials. Later on, the Raëlians moved to Las Vegas, where, it was thought, people were more open-minded.

The Raëlian Movement advocated the use of sex-positive, rather than anti-sex, feminism, the distribution of condoms and other methods of birth control, masturbation, meditation, genetically modified organisms and human cloning, which they saw as the first step towards immortality. The plan was to clone the most beautiful members of the movement first. These chosen few appeared in the October 2004 issue of *Playboy* magazine. In addition, Raël was interested in cloning so that Hitler could be brought back to life to be punished and also to make sure that suicide bombers would not escape justice.

Along with Clonaid – an organization set up for research into cloning – Raël founded Clitaid, a non-profit organization whose aim is to build a 'pleasure hospital' in Burkina Faso to offer medical services for the physical restoration and rehabilitation of victims of female genital mutilation. He fundraised for the cause at the AVN Adult Entertainment Expo in Las Vegas.

Within the movement, there were women's only groups. One of these, the Order of Angels, prioritized sexual gratification and offered their wombs and eggs for cloning experiments. Female supporters were called upon to offer themselves as hostesses for the aliens and Raël, their prophet on earth. Another group, Raël's Girls, comprised women. Seminars begin with 'sensual meditation' and became increasingly sexually adventurous.

Another part of Raëlian belief was the baptism ritual: a guide member would place water upon the forehead of the individual being baptized, and this would give the guide a good understanding of the individual's 'cellular chromosomic plan', which would be judged by the Elohim in the final hour. Baptisms were performed on four specific days a year – 6 August, the anniversary of the bombing of Hiroshima; 13 December, when Raël's first encounter with the Elohim took place; 7 October, when he visited the Elohim's home planet; and the first Sunday in April, when Adam and Eve were created.

According to Raël's words, our solar system, galaxy and universe are tiny particles within the atomic structure of some immense organic being. Within the atoms in the cells of our bodies, he believed there to be minute planetary systems and galaxies inhabited by intelligent creatures like ourselves. The existence of the Elohim proved this, he said.

Raël has found himself in trouble with several governments for following his advocacy of cloning and his emphasis on pleasure in sexual education for children. He has also been accused of plagiarism in his numerous books.

The Raël Movement also ran into controversy over its symbol, which was originally a swastika inside a Star of David. This was modified, the swastika rounded into a 'swirling galaxy'. The official reason given by Raël was that the Elohim had requested this change in order to help the movement obtain permission from the Israeli government to build an extra-terrestrial embassy in Jerusalem. Despite the change, permission for this building project was still denied, and in 2007 the swastika returned as part of the movement's symbol, as, according to Raël, it was 'a symbol of peace for millions of Hindus and Buddhists and for the Raëlians as well, as it is their symbol of infinity in time, their symbol of eternity'.

RAËLISM AND THE BIBLE

According to Raël, the first verse of the Book of Genesis should read: 'In the beginning the Elohim created the heaven and the earth.' The second verse – 'And the Spirit of the Elohim moved upon the face of the waters' – meant that extra-terrestrial reconnaissance flights had begun over the earth, which was completely covered with water and thick mist.

'And the Elohim saw the light was good' apparently meant that the scientists had checked whether light from the Sun was harmful. After more tests, they terraformed a continent – 'Let the waters under the heaven be gathered together into one place, and let the dry land appear'. The vegetable cells were synthesized from chemicals which reproduced – 'Let the earth bring forth grass, the herb yielding seed, and the fruit tree yielding fruit after his kind, whose seed is in itself, upon the earth.' And so on, until the Elohim made humankind in their own image.

There had been a group of scientists who wanted to 'open the eyes' of humankind about their true origins. They were banished to exile on earth as 'serpents'. The rest of the Elohim departed, leaving humans to their own devices.

When the exiled 'serpent' Elohim then began interbreeding with humans, the other Elohim decided to end the experiment and sent nuclear missiles to destroy them. The exiled Elohim told Noah to build a spaceship to preserve what had been created by carrying single cells of the male and female of every species thousands of miles into space. The exploding nuclear missiles of the true Elohim then caused a great tidal wave – a flood – that killed every form of life left on the surface of the earth.

Raëlism holds that the Tower of Babel was not a building but a space rocket, which the true Elohim destroyed, and those with the technical knowledge to build it were scattered across the earth. However, some evil-doers congregated at Sodom and Gomorrah, which then had to be destroyed by atomic bombs. Then, to test that the remaining humans were sufficiently docile, Abraham was asked to sacrifice his son.

The story of Moses and the exodus from Egypt was explained in terms of the intervention of the Elohim. Eventually, Jesus was resurrected by way of a scientific cloning process.

36

SYNANON

From Rehab to Cult

College dropout, former sales executive and barely functioning alcoholic, Charles E. Dederich spent the best part of two decades roaming the USA. After his first divorce, he moved to southern California, where his second wife persuaded him to join Alcoholics Anonymous. Although this proved successful in ending Dederich's alcoholism, the couple subsequently divorced and he began to experiment with LSD. In 1958, using his thirty-three-dollar county welfare cheque, Dederich rented a shop in Ocean Park and tacked up a sign on it which said 'TLC' – the initials of the Tender Loving Care Club. Within a year he renamed the club 'Synanon', which combined '*syn*', meaning 'together', and 'anon', which means 'a person unknown'. He was to bring strangers together, purportedly with the intention of showing them care.

You might have heard the saying, 'Today is the first day of the rest of your life'. It is attributed to Dederich, as it was what he told those joining his drug rehabilitation programme, who were then left to go cold turkey. The treatment offered at Synanon centred on the 'Game', a form of group therapy devised by Dederich. This involved people sitting in a circle and taking their frustrations out on each other. It was confrontational, and what you said did not even have to be true. Sessions lasted for up to forty-eight hours.

The Game formed the basis of the brainwashing that Dederich admitted to using on members of the group later on, though he himself was not adept at it.

To accommodate its swelling membership, Synanon moved into a larger building which housed those on Dederich's programme. The residents of Santa Monica were not happy about having a drug rehabilitation clinic in a residential area and, in 1961, Dederich spent just under a month in jail for zoning violations and running a hospital without a licence. But in the eyes of the members, this made Dederich a martyr, and his apparent persecution made them a more cohesive group.

All things psychological were trendy in the 1960s, and the Synanon house became a fashionable hang-out for celebrities. With recovering jazz musicians in residence, they held the coolest parties on the block. Meanwhile, Dederich was claiming that 80 to 100 per cent of those he treated recovered from their addiction, although he refused government funding for the programme, as taking this would have required him to provide a more official kind of independent verification of its success rate.

To fund the programme, non-addicts were allowed to partake in the therapy offered by the group. From its humble beginnings in 1958, as a treatment centre for forty addicts in a rundown building, by 1967 Synanon boasted 823 members and had moved its premises into Club Casa del Mar, a fashionable beachfront hotel. (It has since been reopened as an upmarket hotel.)

By 1968 a new class of Synanon membership was on offer: that of the Lifestyler. These members were allowed to have jobs outside Synanon and live outside the Synanon community, provided they gave most of their income to the organization. With the money they brought in, Dederich bought land across California to set up new branches of the cult. There was even one established as far away as Detroit.

Dederich soon decided that the Lifestylers did not show enough commitment to the cause. Those who sold their homes and moved in full-time to the premises were allowed to stay, but many of them were forced to leave.

He also changed the rules. Addicts who had been cured of their addiction were no longer allowed to graduate and rejoin the world outside Synanon. Drug addiction, Dederich now propounded, needed a lifetime's cure and a full recovery could only be provided by remaining at Synanon. He started to claim that he was starting a utopian revolution. 'This is the kind of revolution that moved the world from Judaism to Catholicism to Protestantism to Synanism,' he said. 'This is a total revolution game.'

According to Dederich's rules, children and babies were to be taken away from their parents and brought up communally. At first, their parents were to see their children only once a week. But then all the kids were moved to a branch of the cult in Marin County, thereby denying parents all access to them. At this point, members began to leave, and to them Dederich said 'Good riddance!' He believed that those who left had not shown sufficient commitment to the cause. Their choice had been clear: Synanon or their family.

Those who stayed had to do whatever Dederich did. He took LSD, so they had to take it too. He gave up smoking; they had to give it up as well. Dederich then decided he did not want children to be part of the cult at all. Pregnant women were coerced into getting abortions, while men were to have vasectomies – except for Dederich himself, of course. When his wife Betty died, he decided that all the other married couples within his followers should split up. There were over 600 divorces among members the following year.

At this point Synanon had given up running its drug rehabilitation programme, so it could no longer claim to be a not-for-profit organization. Its business interests, which included the creation of promotional ideas and the ownership of petrol stations, were managing to bring in millions of dollars. Dederich decided to establish Synanon and its programme as a religion in order to maintain its tax-exempt status.

Discipline was tightened. Members were accused of being spies and severely beaten. Teenagers were regularly physically abused for insubordination. Devotees were required to shave their heads. In 1978 Synanon spent 200,000 dollars on firearms.

That year, things began to fall apart. Former member Phil Ryan took legal action against Synanon in order to reclaim his daughter, and then two men from the cult beat him senseless on his driveway. He was in a coma for a week.

Attorney Paul Morantz, who had successfully represented a young woman held against her will by the cult, came home on 10 October 1978. When he opened his mailbox, a rattlesnake, whose rattle had been removed to keep it quiet, shot out and bit him. He was rushed to hospital in time to save his life. Two members of the cult were charged with the attempted murder of Morantz. A search of all the Synanon properties unearthed cassette tapes which had recorded Dederich specifically mentioning killing Morantz. He was charged with conspiracy to murder. All three pleaded no contest. The other two went to jail, but Dederich was put on probation after doctors testified that was ill and would die if he were moved to prison without treatment. As part of the legal deal that was struck, he had to step down as head of Synanon.

With its reputation tarnished, interest in the cult dwindled. The Internal Revenue Service removed its tax-exempt status in 1991 and demanded seventeen million dollars in unpaid taxes. Synanon was dissolved of its legal status and its founder declared a bankrupt. Charles E. Dederich died in Visalia, California, in 1997.

SYNANON AND HOLLYWOOD

When film director George Lucas needed a large group of people with shaven heads for the filming of his 1971 science-fiction movie *THX 1138*, he found that most actresses were reluctant to cut off their hair and so he hired some of his extras from among Synanon's members. Robert Altman also hired followers of Synanon as extras for the gambling scenes in his 1974 movie, *California Split*.

The cult had already had released its own film, the eponymous *Synanon*, which starred Edmond O'Brien as Dederich and was released in 1965. It was filmed on location in Santa Monica with the full co-operation of Synanon's leader and members.

Guest speakers at Synanon in 1963 alone included the *Twilight Zone* creator Rod Serling, the legendary science-fiction author Ray Bradbury and the original host of the *Tonight Show*, Steve Allen. Other visitors to Synanon House included Leonard Nimoy, Jane Fonda, Charlton Heston, Milton Berle, the counterculture drug guru Tim Leary, the architect and futurist Buckminster Fuller, and the labour activist Cesar Chavez.

Synanon even got the endorsement of politicians. In 1962 Senator Thomas Dodd from Connecticut said: 'There is indeed a miracle on the beach at Santa Monica.' Jerry Brown, who became Governor of California for the first time in 1975, visited with his father in the mid-1960s. In 1981 Bob Dyan mentioned Synanon in his song 'Lenny Bruce' in the album *Shot of Love*.

37

VOODOO

Servants of the Spirits

Voodoo is associated in popular culture with blood rituals, decapitated chickens, drug-induced trances, dolls with pins stuck in them and, most frightening of all, zombies. In fact, it is a mixture of a number of religions native to West Africa brought to the Caribbean by the slave trade. Its main features are ancestor worship and animism. Instead of a God in heaven, adherents believe that they are the servants of these spirits that exist everywhere in nature. Different forms of Voodoo exist in the various countries slaves were taken from. In some places, Voodoo was mixed with Catholicism, the religion enforced upon the slaves by their masters.

The most widespread form of Voodoo originated in Haiti during its colonization and developed among the African slaves taken there. The name 'Voodoo' derives from the word 'vodun', meaning 'god' or 'spirit' in the language of the Fon people of Benin. Other elements within Voodoo come from the Yoruba and Kongo peoples of West Africa.

The French, in particular, tried to suppress Voodoo. But runaway slaves, known as 'maroons', who set up a resistance movement in the interior, embraced it. During the first slave rebellion in 1758, the maroons wrote the Voodoo Declaration of Independence. In it, the slaves are encouraged to avenge themselves on their white masters. They did this in 1802, under the leadership of François-Dominique Toussaint L'Ouverture, an educated slave who took his inspiration from the French Revolution of 1789. Although he was eventually captured and burned at the stake in France, his legacy was an independent Haiti, where approximately half the population still follow Voodoo.

According to believers, the universe was created by a great snake called Damballah, whose 7,000 coils made the hills and the valleys, and put the stars in the skies. When Damballah shed his skin the waters flowed over the earth. When the sun shone on the water it created a rainbow called Ayido-Wedo, who was so beautiful that Damballah married her.

Busy with his heavenly duties, Damballah left the earth to be tended by 'loas'. There were hundreds of these spirits, and each of them has several names. They come in two types. 'Rada loas' are the good kind. They represent the guardians of custom and tradition. According to the tradition of Voodoo, humans enter into communication with the loas in a very precise manner, as they are capricious and will only be of help if one performs the rituals correctly. Faithful followers build large fires and wear white during their rituals. The loa Ogoun has a very martial energy, and he presides over fire, iron, hunting, politics and war. He is symbolized in ritual by an iron bar placed into the fire .

'Petro loas' are the bad sorts of spirits. They are evoked by the sacrifice of a chicken or a black goat, and can be propitiated by all sorts of fetishes, such as skulls, dog's bones and chicken's feathers. The most famous of all the petro loas is Baron Samedi, Lord of the Graveyard, who, in Hollywood movies at least, is depicted as the leader of the zombies. His symbols are the coffin and the phallus.

Male priests ('houngans') and female priestesses ('mambos') intercede with the loas. The most important part of their rituals is to summon the loa of the crossroads, Legba. He is the only loa who can give permission for the others to leave the spiritual world and enter the material one. Once Legba has been summoned, the houngan prepares the gateway by sprinkling water and waving a sacred sword towards the four cardinal points.

Then the houngan draws a 'vever' (design) on the floor with flour. This will show the symbol of the loa he wants to summon. Each loa has its own symbol. He then strikes the vever with his 'asson' (sacred rattle). This opens the spiritual gateway and the loa he has summoned arrives.

Then the loa is rewarded with its favourite food and drink, which is laid out on the vever. Some petro loas require a blood sacrifice. (Nowadays, not all Voodoo practitioners practise animal sacrifice; but if an animal *is* sacrificed, it is used to provide food for a communal meal after the service.) In the past, the congregation had to drink the blood of the animals slaughtered. It was even said that, in some secret sects, humans were sacrificed and their flesh consumed, but this cannot be verified.

Ostensibly, the most famous element of Voodoo is the zombie: one of the living dead. In fact, zombies as we know them today were largely the creation of Hollywood. In Haiti, the zombie was more of a manifestation of the Christian idea of purgatory. A zombie embodies an in-between state where those who have done wrong in this life are consigned. Voodoo hougans could create zombies – for real – but not through sorcery. They injected victims with a nerve-paralysing toxin from the flesh of the puffer fish. This plunged the victim into a catatonic state for several days, before they were revived with a mild case of amnesia. There was a superstition that robbing a human being of their free will in this way was one way of making the perfect slave.

Voodoo still flourishes, with claims of some forty million followers world-wide. Other forms of Voodoo have evolved in other Caribbean islands. In the English-speaking Caribbean, the darker side of Voodoo has manifested itself as 'obeah', a kind of black magic.

SANTERIA

In Cuba, there is a Catholic strain of Voodoo called Santeria, which means 'the way of the saints'. The saints of the Roman Catholic Church are seen as manifestations of the 'orishas', the gods of the Yoruba tribe. In the past, this was one way slaves could continue to worship their old African gods without falling foul of their Catholic masters. The practice still flourishes in officially atheist Cuba and among Cuban exiles in the United States.

Followers believe that there is one god called Olorun, sometimes Olodumare, and he is the fount of the universe's spiritual energy, which is known as 'ashe'. Olorun communicates to humankind via the orishas, who represent the animistic spirits of nature. Believers contact them through prayer, ritual and sacrifice. The animal being sacrificed is treated with great respect, and its death is regarded as a potent reminder that, one day, all of us will die.

The priests, or 'santeros', must dress entirely in white for a year. They are forbidden from touching or being touched by anyone, looking in the mirror or going out at night during that time. Once initiated, they can hold ceremonies to bestow money and power on others, but their influence is not always benign.

When Panamanian dictator General Manuel Noriega was overthrown by the American invasion of Panama in 1990, an altar to Santeria was found in his office. It was adorned with the effigies of President Reagan and Vice President Bush, who had clearly been cursed. Noriega served a long sentence for drug smuggling in a US federal penitentiary, so one can only suppose that his offers to the gods did not work.

A darker incarnation of Santeria was *Abaqua*: a play of that name produced in Havana in 1978, purporting to show some of cult's rituals – including that of human sacrifice.

Within a fortnight, all the cast members had been tracked down and killed.

In Mexico there is another black-magic version of Santeria called Palo Mayombe, which is sometimes referred to as Santeria's evil twin. Adherents to Palo Mayombe – 'paleros' – must keep the dark spirits in a special locked house. Palero practitioners do not advertise their powers and will only perform spiritual work by referral. Their power is said to be so strong that they can pluck a man from obscurity and turn him into a powerful world figure. Many political leaders have been linked to Palo Mayombe, which is said to keep them in power.

Paleros can make or break a person by saying just a few incantations and by performing minor rituals, and can also bring death to an individual within twenty-four hours. Palo Mayombe has been associated with a number of murders. The Animal Recovery Mission in the USA has documented dogs and cats being confined in small cages and exposed to the extremities of 120-degree heat, with only the blood of other animals to drink, in preparation for ceremonies where they are served as 'food for the gods'.

In 2012 the Animal Recovery Mission discovered a Palo Mayombe shrine in Miami, which housed dressed dolls adorned with beads. Wooden statues of 'gods' with nails embedded in them had been carefully positioned and hand-cuffs draped over them. There were pots filled with trinkets, seashells and seeds, as well as whips made from horse hair. Within feet of the shrine, the carcass of a slaughtered horse was found.

38

MOVE

The Christian Movement for Life

America's Christian Movement for Life – more commonly known as MOVE – was a radical African American group that equated satanic influence with 'the system'. It was led by Vincent Leaphart, a middle-aged black man from West Philadelphia who called himself John Africa. A high-school drop-out, Leaphart could hardly read or write, but along with white middle-class college lecturer Donald J. Glassey, he wrote a 300-page diatribe called *The Teachings of John Africa*, known to followers simply as the 'Book'. Despite it having been written by both a black and a white author, in the fraught atmosphere of race relations in America in the 1970s the 'Book' provided the basis for a militant black organization whose symbol was a clenched fist.

Vincent Leaphart and Donald Glassey met on a protest march in the early 1970s. In 1973 Leaphart established a commune in Glassey's house in the gentrified Powelton Village area of Philadelphia, and by 1975 the commune had swelled to around thirty-five people – both adults and children – and an unspecified number of cats and dogs. The group began protesting, but no one could tell what they were protesting about as the slogans they chanted were largely incoherent. Nevertheless, they managed to disrupt a bicentennial meeting of the governors of the thirteen original states of the Union (of the United States). Glassey then left the group, complaining of their growing talk of violence. He did not get his house back.

Members of MOVE all adopted the surname 'Africa'. The men gave themselves ostentatious titles such as Minister for Information and Minister of Defence. Women got no such exalted positions, and were considered only useful for producing a new wave of MOVE supporters. According to Leaphart's back-to-nature manifesto, after giving birth, his female followers were to cut their umbilical cords with their own teeth and clean their babies with their tongue.

Leaphart controlled every element of his followers' lives, but standards at the commune were starting to slip. The household was grossly overcrowded. It generated a huge amount of garbage that no one ever seemed to clear up. Huge herds of dogs and cats roamed around and naked toddlers wandered in and out at will. The place was becoming a public nuisance and neighbours began to complain. The police were called, but there was little they could do about it.

The idea that they were being watched by the police spawned paranoia among the members. They built a high-security fence and mounted loudspeakers outside so they could taunt the officers. They said they had beaten a child to death, and Leaphart invited the press into the house to show them the dead body. The child had died of natural causes, but at the time it was a propaganda coup – although MOVE's reasons for creating such propaganda are still unclear.

After being arrested for the possession of marijuana, Donald Glassey told the police that MOVE was making bombs. In 1978, under the instruction of the incumbent hard-line mayor, Frank Rizzo, former police chief and scourge of the Black Panthers – police officers were forced to take action. They surrounded the house, while MOVE members appeared in combat fatigues, brandishing rifles and shotguns. When the police stormed the house, they found members of MOVE holding babies and children in front of them as human shields. One policeman was killed in the shoot-out, and three others and four firemen were wounded. Nine MOVE members found themselves behind bars for life, but Leaphart was not one of them. He had slipped out of the house before the bullets had started flying.

The police caught up with him three years later, in 1981, in Richmond, Virginia. He stood trial for firearms charges that had been outstanding since the Philadelphia siege in 1978, but was acquitted. Leaphart moved into his sister's house in the Cobbs Creek area of Philadelphia and began building up the commune again. Soon the situation was much like it had been before the shoot-out in 1978, but this time he had the windows of the house boarded up and a pill-box built on the roof.

When a man armed with a shotgun appeared on the roof of the building where the commune lived, the police decided it was time to act. On 8 August 1985, on the anniversary of the 1978 shoot-out, more than 300 policemen and fire-fighters camped out around MOVE's new headquarters. They maintained a siege for eight months, watching as members brought out goods from the reinforced bunker they were now excavating in the cellar. Doubting the legality of any direct assault on the house, however, the new African American mayor, Wilson Goode, stayed the police's hand. In negotiations, MOVE conceded they wanted to be allowed out, but demanded the release of all MOVE members sentenced after the 1978 siege.

As voices through the MOVE loudspeakers continued to taunt the police and threaten death to anyone who approached the house, the surrounding houses were evacuated. Police sharp-shooters sheltered behind sandbags as fire-engines drove into position. Police Commissioner Gregory Sambor gave MOVE members one last chance to give themselves up, saying that they had fifteen minutes to come out with their hands held up. MOVE's response was to suggest that the police personnel check their life assurance, reminding them that one policeman had lost his life in 1978.

At 6 a.m. on 13 May 1985, the battle began. High-pressure fire hoses were turned on the roof-top pill-box. It withstood the blast. Tear-gas grenades lobbed into the compound drew automatic fire in response. Police started drilling through the wall of the house next door. MOVE members fired through the wall and the police responded by firing machine guns.

An explosive charge was laid, but it was not enough to breach the wall. A second explosion made a small hole, but then the police's tear-gas generator broke down. The police broke through the adjoining wall at the other side of the house more easily and threw in tear-gas grenades. When the police followed their grenades through into the commune's house, one officer was hit by gunfire. His flak-jacket saved his life, but when news of this filtered back up the chain of command the action to seize control of the house was called off. Their guns fell quiet at around 7.20 a.m. By this time the police had loosed off over 10,000 rounds of ammunition, but they were no further forward. Mayor Goode held his head in his hands.

The police were at a loss as to what to do. They fetched a crane and wrecking ball to knock the house down, but could not get the crane down the narrow street, and the police commissioner found no volunteers who wanted to operate it, in any case. The stand-off continued for the rest of the day. The families of MOVE members used a bull-horn speaker to beg their loved ones to come out. There was no response. Soon after 5 p.m., the fateful decision was made: the police were going to bomb the building. This was unprecedented. Never before had the American civil authorities dropped a bomb on a home. The idea was to dislodge the roof-top pillbox, blow a hole in the roof and pump in tear-gas. But the police sadly misjudged their mission. They packed a bag with a commercial explosive used in mining and, at around 5.30 p.m., they dropped it from a helicopter onto the roof of the house.

THE RESULTING FIRE

The explosion sent wreckage flying ten metres into the air. Some of the huge crowd that had gathered around cheered, but the cheers were mixed with cries of horror. The authorities are bombing babies, people said. When the dust cleared, the pillbox was still standing – the explosive had not been powerful enough to break it. But worse still, explosives had set a nearby house on fire. Soon flames were leaping a hundred feet up into the air, but fire-fighters could not move in because MOVE members kept up a withering barrage of gunfire. Police snipers tried to pick off the gunmen they saw silhouetted against the flames. At the back of the house, a thirty-year-old woman and a thirteen-year-old boy managed to escape. With the police providing intense fire to cover the two of them, they were rescued and arrested. They were the only ones who got out alive.

By the time the fire brigade had got the fire under control, the entire block had burned down and the fire had spread to adjoining streets. In all, nearly sixty houses were gutted. In the cellar of the MOVE headquarters, among the charred remains of dogs and children, the police eventually found what they were looking for: the body of John Africa.

39

THE GERMAN BRETHREN

The New Baptists

The German Baptist Brethren, or German Brethren, are a sect of American Baptists who originated in Germany. They are sometimes known as New Baptists to distinguish them from other Baptist groups, and their members are popularly called 'Dunkers', 'Dunkards', or 'Tunkers', from the German word *tunken* – 'to dip' – as initiates are baptized by being immersed in water three times. The sect was founded in 1708 in Schwarzenau, in North Rhine-Westphalia, when Baptists there broke away from the Lutheran and Reformed churches to follow a more literal interpretation of the scriptures. They were led by the religious dissenter Alexander Mack, who expected the imminent return of Christ.

The new German Brethren were barely established in Germany when religious persecution forced the brethren to take refuge among the Mennonites, a Protestant sect, based in northern Holland. From there the German Baptist Brethren emigrated to Pennsylvania, in small groups, between 1719 and 1733.

The first congregation was established in America on Christmas Day of 1723 by Peter Becker at Germantown, Pennsylvania. There, in 1743, Christopher Sauer, one of the sect's first pastors, printed a Bible in German – the first Bible published in a European language in America. From Pennsylvania, the German Baptist

Brethren's creed migrated westwards to states including Maryland, Virginia, Ohio, Indiana, Illinois, Iowa, Missouri, Nebraska, Kansas and North Dakota.

Doctrinal differences sprang up as the church spread and gained new members, but followers held on to the core beliefs propagated by Mack. He said he could not find any reference to the baptism of infants in the New Testament, so he rejected it. He also believed in one God, in the form of the trinity of Father, Son and Holy Spirit – hence the German Brethren's practice of triple immersion, whereby the adult initiate was immersed in the baptismal water, face down, three times, in the name of the Father, the Son and the Holy Spirit. This practice gave the sect its nickname 'Dompelaers' – Pennsylvania Dutch for 'tumblers'.

The German Brethren believe that the New Testament is the infallible guide to all spiritual matters. It is the Word of God, revealed through Jesus Christ and, inspired by him, through the Apostles as well. Consequently, their celebration of the Communion service has to follow exactly the way it was originally performed by Christ, which means it is celebrated in the evening and all communicants are seated at a common table. Communion is accompanied by the love feast, the ceremony of the washing of feet in imitation of Jesus Christ washing his disciples' feet and the holy kiss. This is observed by the sexes separately.

The German Baptist Brethren pray over their sick and anoint them with oil. In most matters they are rigid non-resisters – that is, they will not resist authority even when it is being unjustly exercised. However, they will not bear arms or study the art of war; they refuse to take oaths and will not sue others in civil courts.

In 1782 the sect forbade its members from owning slaves. They eschewed liquor and tobacco and advocated simple dress. The sect originally opposed voting or taking any active part in political affairs, even to the extent of encouraging members to boycott taking part in the population census, but in contemporary society these restrictions have mostly disappeared, and the

German Baptist Brethren's past prejudice against higher education has now been relaxed.

An early secession from the general body of the Dunkers was a group known as the Seventh-Day Dunkers, a group who believed, as did the Seventh-Day Adventists of Chapter 17, that the seventh day, Saturday, was the true Sabbath. Their founder was Johann Conrad Beissel, who founded the Seventh-Day Dunkers in 1725, before returning to live as a hermit in a cave on the Cocalico Creek in Pennsylvania. During his time as leader, he established a semi-monastic community called the 'Order of the Solitary'. The group gradually abandoned these early strains of monasticism, and in 1814 they were incorporated as the Seventh-Day Baptists.

In 1880 the 'old order' Dunkers began to pull out of the German Brethren. They opposed Sunday Schools, revival meetings and the missionary work the brethren were undertaking in Asia Minor, India and several European countries. They continued to oppose higher education and their participation in the census. Determined to preserve the 'ancient order' of church ordinances, worship and dress, they formed the Old German Baptist Brethren in 1881.

The following year, the radicals, or progressives, formed the evangelical Brethren Church. They objected to a distinctive form of dress and to the supremacy of the annual conferences that lay down the rules of worship and members' way of life. Meanwhile, the bulk of the adherents continued as the original German Baptist Brethren, until they rechristened themselves the Church of the Brethren in 1908.

In 1913 a number of followers living in California and Indiana removed themselves from the Old German Baptist Brethren. Then in 1921, those living near Dayton, Ohio, also broke away from the Old German Baptist Brethren. Attempts to reunite them during the years 1929 to 1930 failed, with the Old Brethren German Baptists making a more solid base for themselves in the area around Camden, Indiana. There was a further split when a still more conservative group who called themselves the German Baptist Brethren broke away from the Old German Baptist Brethren. Then in 2009 another schism occurred with the establishment of the Old German Baptist Brethren, New Conference sect.

In 1939 there was a schism among the progressives when the National Fellowship of Brethren Churches broke with the evangelical Brethren Church whose headquarters were in Ashland, Ohio. The National Fellowship of Brethren Churches then became the Fellowship of Grace Brethren Churches – a.k.a the Grace Brethren Church – with headquarters at Winona Lake, Indiana.

Members of the Church of the Brethren, Conservative Grace Brethren Churches, the German Baptist Brethren, the Fellowship of Grace Brethren Churches, Old German Baptist Brethren and the Brethren Church got together for the Brethren World Assembly in 2003, representing some 600,000 members from around the world.

THE BRETHREN CARD

In 1923 the annual conference of the Church of the Brethren approved a statement of faith, commonly known as the 'Brethren Card'. It stated:

1. This body of Christians originated early in the eighteenth century, the church being a natural outgrowth of the Pietistic movement following the Reformation.
2. [This religion] firmly accepts and teaches the fundamental evangelical doctrines of:
   - the inspiration of the Bible
   - the personality of the Holy Spirit
   - the Virgin Birth
   - the deity of Christ
   - the sin-pardoning value of his atonement
   - his resurrection from the tomb, ascension and personal and visible return, and

- the resurrection, both of the just and unjust (John 5:28–9; 1 Thess. 4:13–18).
3. Observes the following New Testament rites:
   - Baptism of penitent believers by trine immersion for the remission of sins (Matt. 28:19; Acts 2:38)
   - Feet-washing (John 13:1–20; 1 Tim. 5:10)
   - Love feast (Luke 22:20; John 13:4; 1 Cor. 11:17–34; Jude 12)
   - Communion (Matt. 26:26–30)
   - the Christian salutation (Rom. 16:16; Acts 20:37)
   - proper appearance in worship (1 Cor. 11:2–16)
   - the anointing for healing in the name of the Lord (James 5:13–18; Mark 6:13)
   - the laying-on of hands (Acts 8:17; 19:6; 1 Tim. 4:14).
   These rites are representative of spiritual facts which obtain in the lives of true believers, and as such are essential factors in the development of the Christian life.
4. Emphasizes:
   - daily devotion for the individual, and family worship for the home (Eph. 6:18–20; Philipp. 4:8, 9)
   - stewardship of time, talents and money (Matt. 25:14–30)
   - taking care of the fatherless, widows, poor, sick and aged (Acts 6:1–7)
5. Opposes on scriptural grounds:
   - War and the taking of human life (Matt. 5:21–6, 43, 44; Rom. 12:19–21; Isa. 53:7–12)
   - violence in personal and industrial controversy (Matt. 7:12; Rom. 13:8–10)
   - intemperance in all things (Titus 2:2; Gal, 5:19–26; Eph. 5:18)
   - going to law, especially against our Christian brethren (1 Cor. 6:1–9)

- divorce and remarriage, except for the one scriptural reason (Matt. 19:9)
- every form of oath (Matt. 5:33–7; James 5:12)
- membership in secret oath-bound societies (2 Cor. 6:14–18)
- games of chance and sinful amusements (1 Thess. 5:22; 1 Peter 2:11; Rom. 12:17)
- extravagant and immodest dress (1 Tim. 2:8–10; 1 Peter 3:1–6).

6. Labours earnestly, in harmony with the Great Commission:
   - for the evangelization of the world
   - for the conversion of men to Jesus Christ; and
   - for the realization of the life of Jesus Christ in every believer (Matt. 28:18–20; Mark 16:15, 16; 2 Cor. 3:18).

7. Maintains the New Testament as its only creed, in harmony with which the above brief doctrinal statement is made.

40

THE FEDERATION OF DAMANHUR

The Temples of Humankind

Located in Chiusella Valley in the foothills of the Alps in north-west Italy, the Federation of Damanhur is a commune of over a thousand people. It has its own currency and constitution, schools, university, daily newspaper and publishing house. Its ethical and spiritual foundations are broadly based upon New Age, neo-Pagan and other ancient religions' beliefs and they are made manifest in a vast underground complex called the Temples of Humankind. The sect is named after the city of Damanhur in Lower Egypt. This city was also known as the city of Horus in Ancient Egypt, named after the sky god with the body of a man and the head of a falcon.

The federation was the brainchild of Oberto Airaudi, a writer and artist born in Turin in 1950. From an early age, he said he had mastered telekinesis, managing to roll eggs across the kitchen floor by the power of thought alone. He said he conjured up ghostly apparitions to frighten his opponents on the football pitch and attached rockets to the sides of his bicycle to see if he could fly.

At the age of ten, he claims he experienced visions of what he believed to be a past life. There he had visited amazing temples. Around them he dreamed that there lived a highly evolved community of people working for the common good, enjoying an idyllic existence. The temples in his visions were underground, so he practised excavation by digging a hole under his parents' house.

Airaudi also claimed to have had a supernatural gift for 'remote viewing': the ability to travel in his mind's eye to describe in detail the contents of the buildings that he saw. 'My goal was to recreate the temples from my visions,' he said.

By the age of fourteen, he was experimenting with hypnosis, levitation and out-of-body travel, giving lectures on physics, maths, music and esoteric philosophy to crowds of between eighty and a hundred people. He was convinced he was on to something when two Jesuit teachers left their order to study under his tutelage.

Airaudi opened a centre in Turin which was named after Horus, supported by the proceeds of a successful insurance business, psychic healing courses and prana-therapy yogic well-being clinics he ran all over Italy. He then took the name Falco, naming himself after the Italian word for falcon.

One of his research projects was studying 'synchronic lines', a system of energy channels that encircle the globe. 'Synchronic lines are like rivers in which an infinite amount of knowledge is stored,' he said, 'as if they were a library containing all that humankind has ever thought.' Where these lines intersect, he said, there exist supercharged regions he called 'shining knots', which served as access points to the system. One was in Tibet; another was in Valchiusella, or the Chiusella Valley.

In 1977 Falco and a dozen of his students moved there. One summer night in 1978, they were sitting around a campfire when they saw a shooting star overhead. This they took as a sign. Soon after they started digging and began work on the temple which they planned to build under a nearby hillside. The work was done in secret and the entrance was camouflaged.

Seventy or eighty Damanhurians worked on the subterranean temple for thirteen years. Then, in 1992, a disgruntled ex-member turned them in to the authorities, complaining that they had no planning permission for the construction. Soldiers arrived in helicopters and threatened to dynamite the mountain unless Falco and his followers divulged the hidden location of the temples.

Falco duly complied and opened the hidden door to the Blue Temple, a circular chamber 8 metres in diameter which was decorated with elaborate murals and mosaics. There were nine of these huge underground chambers, a tenth of what Falco had planned. They were linked by secret doors and hundreds of metres of richly decorated tunnels: the compound was almost double the size of Big Ben.

The public prosecutor who entered the Temples of Humankind could hardly believe his eyes. The walls bore testament to cosmic histories and panoramic visions of the birth and evolution of the universe, along with allegorical scenes of war between good and evil in the hearts of men. There were mosaics and statues of the gods and goddesses of Greece and Rome, Sumer and Babylon, of Hindus and Zulus, of Aztecs and Algonquin Indians. And everywhere there were motifs of Egypt and Atlantis – shifting sands and swimming dolphins, warriors and dragons, scarabs and hieroglyphs, Osiris, Anubis and the falcons of Horus.

'They are to remind people that we are all capable of much more than we realize and that hidden treasures can be found within every one of us once you know how to access them,' said Falco.

Amazingly, the complex was entirely the work of a group of lay people. None of them architects, none of them engineers, none of them even professional artists.

'I had a very big head, so I thought I could do it,' Falco said. 'In the Middle Ages, they built cathedrals without being engineers or architects. So if they made such things, why not us?'

Due to the Pagan imagery, the Catholic Church urged the authorities to have the Temples destroyed, but the Damanhurians fought a long court battle to preserve their work. They collected signatures worldwide and invited television crews and journalists to visit the site. After four years, with the support of the Beaux

Arts Authority, a body which regulated art and architecture, they won. Italian law was amended to legalize the underground structure, with the government declaring the Temples of Humankind to be the eighth wonder of the world. It was to be saved, but no more chambers were to be built there. However, new work was planned at an abandoned stone quarry nearby.

Federation members live in forty small communities comprising ten to twenty people each. Another 400 live in the vicinity of the temples and participate in activities there. The federation owns over a thousand acres of woodland, farming land and residential development. There are also another one hundred privately owned buildings, studios, workshops, small businesses and farms. The Federation of Damanhur owns more houses and land near Florence as well, where its members grow olive trees.

Damanhurians have served on the local council in Valchiusella and one has been elected mayor of the nearby town of Vidracco. In an effort to regenerate the region, the federation bought an abandoned Olivetti factory that had closed down twenty years earlier. The building was converted to house schools, an adult-education centre, a research lab for molecular biology, an organic food store, a renewable energy and bio-architecture consultancy firm, fashion and jewellery stores, art and restoration studios, craft workshops, an art gallery, a café and a conference centre.

Members of the commune work at the Red Cross station in Vidracco serve as volunteer fire-fighters, take care of the elderly and provide transport for hospitals and private citizens. In 2005 the United Nations gave the Federation of Damanhur an award for being a model for a new sustainable society. For outsiders, it offers short residential courses, which include a visit to the Temples of Humankind, and hospitality is provided in exchange for work in the community. Their arts festival is open to summer guests and there are theatrical, dance and musical performances in Valchiusella. There is also a housing project for families and groups who want to settle in the valley.

THE FIRST ARTICLES OF THE CONSTITUTION

- Citizens are brothers and sisters who help one another through reciprocal trust, respect, clarity, acceptance, solidarity and continuous inner transformation.
- Everyone is committed to always giving others opportunities to aim higher.
- Each citizen makes a commitment to spread positive, harmonious thoughts and to direct every thought action towards spiritual growth.
- Through community life, Damanhur aims at developing individuals whose reciprocal relations are regulated by knowledge and consciousness. The fundamental rules of life are common sense, thinking well of others and the welcoming and exaltation of diversity.

41

SKOPTSY

The Castrated Ones

The Skoptsy were an offshoot of the Khlysty, which you might remember from Chapter 29. To avoid the sin of lust, male followers would castrate themselves, partially or completely, while the women would have their breasts removed and sometimes undergo female genital mutilation. While only male castration is mentioned in the Bible, the human genitals were seen as the mark of Cain, and Adam and Eve were said to have had the halves of the forbidden fruit grafted onto their bodies, forming testicles and breasts. In this way the removal of these body parts were believed to restore the Skoptsy to the pristine state of humanity before original sin. Although the Russian authorities made repeated attempts to stamp out the castration cult, it persisted into the twentieth century.

In 1771 in Orel, Russia, a peasant named Andrei Ivanov was convicted of having persuaded thirteen other peasants to castrate themselves. He was savagely beaten and exiled to Siberia. His assistant, Kondraty Selivanov, fled, but was captured in 1775 and also sent to Siberia. However, with the help of other followers, Selivanov managed to escape.

Two years later he moved to St Petersburg. In an interview with Tsar Paul, Selivanov told the Tsar that he was the Son of God incarnated in the person of Peter III, Paul's father, who had been overthrown and assassinated in 1762. Peter had been popular both among the schismatics (those who might cause division in the Russian Orthodox church) because he granted them liberty of conscience, and among the peasants because he had divided the church's land among labourers. The Tsar was not impressed, however, and Selivanov was imprisoned in a madhouse.

He was released under Paul I's successor, Alexander I, in 1802 and for eighteen years lived in the home of a follower in St Petersburg. Selivanov claimed the title 'God of Gods and King of Kings' for himself, and said he had secured the salvation of believers through a self-inflicted mutilation. Followers called themselves 'God's Lambs' or 'White Doves' and maintained that they were fulfilling Christ's counsel of perfection according to St Matthew's gospel. When a disciple asked Jesus whether a man should marry, he replied: 'Not all men can receive this precept, but only those to whom it is given. For there are some eunuchs, which were so born from their mother's womb: and there are some eunuchs, which were made eunuchs of men: and there be eunuchs, which have made themselves eunuchs for the Kingdom of Heaven's sake. He that is able to receive it, let him receive it.' (Matthew 19:12).

Again, according to the apostle Matthew, Jesus had said: 'I say to you that everyone who looks at a woman lustfully has already committed adultery with her in his heart. If your right eye causes you to sin, pluck it out and throw it away; it is better that you lose one of your members than that your whole body is thrown into hell. And if your right hand causes you to sin, cut it off and throw it away . . .' (Matthew 5:28).

The Skoptsy believed that Jesus had been castrated, which was why he never married. And they interpreted the ceremony of his washing of the disciples' feet as a symbolic, if not actual castration of the apostles.

The castration was performed in stages. First the testicles were removed; then the penis would be removed. In some cases, the pectoral muscles were cut into, and the shoulders, back and legs sometimes mutilated as well. This was done, apparently, so that angels' wings could sprout from the wounds. The process was called the 'baptism of fire', and the aim was not to make the human race extinct, but rather to perfect the individual.

The earliest records of female mutilation dates from 1815. In one ceremony, it was said, the left breast of a girl of fifteen or sixteen was excised in a warm bath. Afterwards, the assembly took communion, eating the raw flesh after it had been cut into fine pieces. Both breasts were often cut off in these ceremonies, sometimes along with the outer parts of the female genitalia.

Skoptsy meetings were held late at night in cellars, and lasted until dawn. Men wore long, wide, white shirts with a girdle and baggy white trousers. Women also dressed in white. All present either wore white stockings or went barefoot. Their ceremonies include hymn-singing, addresses and ecstatic dancing similar to that of the Khlysty.

But when army officers and upper-class men had themselves castrated, the Tsar was asked to step in to stop the practice and this sect. In 1820 Selivanov was arrested again and shut up in a monastery at Sùzdal, where he died in 1832 at the age of 100.

However, Skoptsism did not die out with Selivanov. Noblemen, military and naval officers, civil servants, priests and merchants continued to join its ranks, though not all of them mutilated themselves. However, between 1847 and 1866, 515 male and 240 female adherents were transported to Siberia, and in 1872 trials of Skoptsy adherents took place all over Russia. Nevertheless, two years after that, the sect still numbered at least 5,444 members.

The government attempted to ridicule members of the sect by forcing them to dress in women's clothing and be paraded as a laughing stock. When that failed, a further 130 Skoptsy were sentenced to transportation in 1876. To escape prosecution, some immigrated, generally to Romania. But although the law in Russia was strict — every eunuch was compelled to register — Skoptsism still continued to flourish well into the twentieth century.

The Skoptsy were millenarians and awaited a Messiah, whom they believed would establish an empire of the saints on earth among those who had made themselves pure. However, the Messiah would not come till the Skoptsy numbered 144,000 followers, and so they directed all their efforts to reaching this total. Simple persuasion was not enough, and bribery and force were often used. Children were bought from poor parents, mutilated and brought up in the faith.

The sect was thought to have died out completely under Stalin's rule, although there are still reports of anti-sexual religious ascetics who favour self-castration.

RELIGIOUS CASTRATION

The Skoptsy are not the only sect to have practised religious castration. At the end of the third century BC, tree worship came to the Romans in the form of the cult of Cybele, the Great Mother Goddess. Her consort – and, in some versions of the tale, her son – was Attis. When Cybele and Attis were to be married, his hermaphroditic father Agdistis grew jealous and cursed Attis, who castrated himself and bled to death. Agdistis was overcome with guilt and begged Zeus to prevent Attis's body from decaying. The plea was successful and Attis was reborn as the sacred and evergreen pine tree.

During Hannibal's invasion of Italy in 204 BC, the Romans turned to the Sybilline Books (these were books of prophecy consulted by the Roman Senate in times of emergencies) and revealed that if they brought the symbol of Cybele – a small black meteorite – to Rome, all the way from the home of the cult in Pessinus, in Asia Minor, victory would be theirs. That is what they did and Hannibal was defeated in 202 BC.

However, the Romans were horrified by the rites of Cybele which were associated with the stone. Each year, followers cut a pine tree from the forest and erected it in the temple.

On the Day of Blood, new priests would castrate themselves in front of it. Older priests would let their own blood, while other followers would slash themselves with knives so that their blood splashed on to the tree. Some believers also castrated themselves during an ecstasy of drumming and dancing. Romans were forbidden to join in, but many enjoyed watching the gory spectacle.

Later self-castration was replaced with the gory rite of the Taurobolium. Initiates to the cult would sit in a pit covered with a wooden grate. A bull, adorned in gold, would be sacrificed on top of the grate so that its blood would be splashed over the initiates below, baptizing them in it. This practice continued until the fourth century AD, when the first Christian Roman emperor, Constantine, banned human and animal sacrifice across the empire.

42

THE REICHSBÜRGER MOVEMENT

Citizens of the German Reich

The Reichsbürgerbewegung, or Reich Citizens' Movement, rejects the legitimacy of the modern Federal Republic of Germany. Instead, members claim to be citizens of the German Reich as it existed within its pre-Second World War borders in 1937, before the German annexation of Austria and the Sudetenland. Others look back to the German Empire, or the Second Reich, following unification in 1871. Present-day members refuse to pay federal taxes, and they print their own passports and driving licences. The Bundesamt für Verfassungsschutz, the Federal Office for the Protection of the Constitution, estimated that there were some 18,000 Reichsbürgers in Germany in 2018. Many of these ascribe to right-wing populist, anti-Semitic and Nazi ideologies.

Reichsbürgers maintain that the German Reich is governed by a Kommissarische Reichsregierung (a provisional Reich government) or by an Exilregierung (a government in exile). They believe that the 1919 Weimar Constitution is still in effect and the Federal Republic of Germany as it exists today is merely the successor state to West Germany, which was created in 1949 by the Western powers who had occupied Germany in 1945. According to Reichsbürgers, Nazi Germany did not formally surrender to the Allies and so Germany is still at war and under occupation.

The original Kommissarische Reichsregierung was formed in 1985 by Wolfgang Gerhard Günter Ebel, a former railway superintendent from West Berlin who appointed himself Reich Chancellor. Members of his cabinet soon fell out with him, however, and left to start their own provisional governments, including the Exilregierung Deutsches Reich or the Deutsches Reich AG (German Reich AG).

Under Ebel's leadership the Kommissarische Reichsregierung issued building permits and other 'official' documents, along with currency and stamps for the regime. His government claims to have issued a thousand arrest warrants to those who have disregarded Kommissarische Reichsregierung documents, threatening to have them tried for high treason – the penalty for which would be death – when his government came into power. Later attempts to have Ebel prosecuted for impersonating a public official failed because the courts found him to be certifiably insane.

Reichsbürgers are mostly men in their fifties who come from socially disadvantaged sections of society. A district court judge in Saxony-Anhalt described them as 'conspiracy theorists' and 'malcontents'. And they are dangerous. The group have allegedly been trying to build an army in preparation for a 'day of reckoning': an imagined day of reckoning or uprising against the German government.

More than a thousand members have at least one gun licence and police have found large caches of weapons and ammunition in searches. Reichsbürgers have shot at the police during raids, arguing they had the right to defend their property. In 2014 a similar group calling itself the 'Free State of Prussia' attempted to build up its own militia by smuggling in arms from outside the country.

One Reichsbürger, Adrian Ursache – a former winner of the Mr Germany beauty pageant – was charged with attempted murder after shooting and injuring an officer during a special police force raid on 25 August 2016. While awaiting trial he was divorced by a former Miss Germany.

On 19 October 2016, a self-proclaimed Reichsbürger fired on a special response unit of the Bavarian police in Georgensgmünd, when they attempted to confiscate his thirty-one firearms after his gun licence had been revoked. Three police officers were badly hurt, and one of them died later from his injuries. On 23 October 2017 the perpetrator, known only as Wolfgang P., was sentenced to life imprisonment.

After busting a human-trafficking ring in northern Germany in May 2018, police discovered that at least one of the main suspects in the ring was involved in the Reichsbürgerbewegung. The Reich Citizens Movement has even infiltrated the police itself: a Bavarian police officer was suspended from duty due to his connections to the movement, and police officers in other states are suspected of having similar connections.

Some members of the movement have retaliated against the state by turning to modes of civil disobedience, filing floods of motions and objections in response to court orders. Regardless of the deliberate time-wasting purpose of these complaints, the authorities are required to process every formal request they receive. Mayors from a number of communities have protested that, above and beyond having to deal with so much senseless work, they have also been attacked by Reichsbürger members, both verbally and physically. Members often film such attacks and post the footage online.

One of the more extreme Reichsbürgers was former chef Peter Fitzek, who declared himself King of Germany in 2012 and installed his 'kingdom' in an abandoned hospital in the East German town of Wittenberg. A video of his bizarre coronation was posted online.

As the self-styled Peter the First, he garnered thousands of followers, and he urged his 'subjects' to deposit their money into savings accounts in an illegal national bank which he had opened. Almost 600 people deposited €1.7 million into this bank. Fitzek spent €1.3 million of it.

Faced with embezzlement charges, he claimed in court that he had used the money for the good of his community. Judge Ursula Mertens retorted: 'You, Mr Fitzek, have done nothing for the common good. You have used the money on yourself.'

He was sentenced to three years and eight months in prison. It was not the first time Fitzek had run into trouble with the law. In 2016 he had been caught driving without a proper licence for the eighth time, and claimed that he had abandoned it in favour of one he had authorized himself. He had also been previously convicted of running an illegal health insurance scheme.

Another prominent member of the Reichsbürgerbewegung is the R&B singer Xavier Naidoo. His invitation to represent Germany at the 2016 Eurovision Song Contest was withdrawn following an online petition condemning his anti-semetic and homophobic lyrics. His 2012 song 'Wo *sind*' ('Where Are') was widely criticized in Germany for implying all homosexuals were paedophiles. In another song released after the 2008 financial crisis, Naidoo referred to the banker Baron Rothschild as 'Baron Deadschild' and called him a 'schmock', a derogatory term in Yiddish.

THE SOVEREIGN CITIZEN MOVEMENT

In the US, adherents of the sovereign citizen movement refuse to acknowledge the federal citizenship bestowed to former slaves after the Civil War under the Fourteenth Amendment to the constitution. They refuse to pay federal taxes and, like their German counterparts, bombard the courts with paperwork.

One of the conspirators in the 1995 Oklahoma City bombing which killed at least 168 people was a member of the sovereign citizen movement. In 2010 two members shot and killed two policemen who had stopped their car in West Memphis, Arkansas. Another was found guilty of threatening to arrest the Mayor of Kirkland, Washington, after he was caught driving on a suspended licence with a gun and ammunition on the back seat.

Although members of the sovereign citizen movement do not recognize the US dollar as it is federal currency, in 2011 two members were jailed after being convicted in a money-laundering scheme. The following year two more members were jailed for tax fraud. Others have used sovereign citizen arguments as a defence in cases as diverse as murder, kidnapping, sexual abuse and blowing up a gas pipeline.

The movement has also spread to Australia, where the authorities in New South Wales consider it to be a potential terrorist threat. It is estimated that there were as many as 300 sovereign citizens in the state in 2015.

In 2011 sovereign citizen Malcolm Roberts sent a bizarre affidavit to the then Australian Prime Minister Julia Gillard in which he demanded to be made exempt from the carbon tax, using language consistent with the movement. In 2016 Roberts was elected as senator for Queensland in the 2016 Australian federal election, but he was later found to be ineligible for office because he had not renounced his British citizenship before his nomination.

43

ODINISM

Reconstructing the Heathen Tradition

Odinism is one of the many names given to the attempt to reconstruct the pre-Christian religion of northern Europe. It takes its name from Odin, the supreme god in Norse mythology. Modern Heathen groups reviving the ancient practices of the peoples of Anglo-Saxon England, Scandinavia and Germany call their religion by various names, including: Asatru, the Northern Tradition, Odalism, Forn Sed, Germanic Pagan Reconstructionism, Germanic Neopaganism, Fyrnsidy, Theodism or, simply, Heathenry. In Iceland, Heathenry has once again become an official religion. The majority of Heathens are middle-aged and of European descent, and there are more men than women. Many are often involved in other Pagan religions, such as Wicca or Druidry, and take part in re-enactments that can blur the distinction between real life and fantasy.

The foundation of modern Heathenry is derived from a range of sources, such as medieval Icelandic stories known as Eddas and Sagas, Anglo-Saxon poetry such as *Beowulf*, German texts such as the *Nibelungenlied*, the works of the eighth-century English monk St Bede and *Germania* by the Roman historian Tacitus. Some Heathens are inspired by the use of quasi-Nordic mythology in more modern literature such as J. R. R. Tolkein's trilogy *Lord of the Rings*, and, indeed, the Pagan imagery in the lyrics of much heavy metal music. Archaeological evidence is also used to build a picture of the original Heathen religion.

Like most early religions, Odinism is polytheistic, recognizing a large number of gods and other spiritual entities. Most of these are known by the Anglicized versions of their Old Norse names. The god called Odhinn in Old Norse was known as Wodhanaz to early Germanic tribes, Woden in Anglo-Saxon and Old Saxon, and Wuotan in Old High German. Some of the better-known Heathen gods are preserved in the names of the English days of the week: Tuesday is named after Tiw or Tyr, Wednesday after Woden or Odin, Thursday after Thunor or Thor, and Friday after the goddess Frige or Freyja.

Alongside them are other spiritual beings such as the Disir – female ancestral spirits attached to a tribe, family or individual – and the Norns – three female entities who weave the web of 'wyrd', the fabric that holds the universe together. Then there are 'hidden folk': elves, brownies, dwarves and ettins. These beings interact with other supernatural entities such as the housewights that live in homes and the landwights who occupy features of the landscape such as streams, mountains, forests or fields. Heathen outdoor rituals cannot proceed until permission has been obtained from the landwights.

Borrowing from Norse mythology, Heathens believe that the world we inhabit is just one of nine realms that are part of a cosmological tree. Dwarves live in one realm, and elves, giants and divinities in the others. According to Heathen mythology, gods are not immortal. A number will die in a series of disasters, including in a great battle called the Twilight of the Gods. After that, the world will re-emerge renewed. The surviving gods will return and the two remaining human beings will repopulate the earth.

Heathenry has no unified organization or central authority to regulate its beliefs and practices. The movement comprises small groups, known as kindreds or hearths, whose members are often from the same family. There is no recognized priesthood, though some members act as 'godhis' and 'gydhjas' – priests and priestesses.

Feasts and celebrations are held to mark the passing of the seasons, weddings or baby-naming ceremonies. These vary from group to group, but the three major Heathen festivals are Winter Nights – usually celebrated in October or November to mark the beginning of winter; Yule – a twelve-day festival that begins around the time of the winter solstice; and a spring festival in honour of the Anglo-Saxon goddess Eostre.

The principal rite is the 'blot'. In the past this involved the sacrifice of an animal and the sharing of the meat. In a modern blot, a place is set for the god, ancestor or elf, and an offering of food or drink is made. If the blot is held outdoors, the offering is thrown on the fire.

A 'symbel' is a drinking ceremony, in which drinking horns are filled with mead and toasts are made. In the first round the toast is made to a god, in the second to an ancestor, and subsequent rounds are made to anything participants suggest. A separate libation is poured out as an offering to the gods, or to the local housewrights or landwights. To appease the hidden folk, cakes and ale are left in a special bowl in the house, while other food and drink is left outside at a small garden altar.

Some ancient Northern European magical practices have been rediscovered by Heathens, such as the carving of runes on to talismans and the chanting of charms called 'galdor'. Modern Heathens practise runic divination, and they have revived a shamanistic practice known as 'seidh'. This usually involves drumming to induce a trance, although some Heathens use psychoactive drugs to the same end. In an 'oracular seidh', a seer answers questions or gives advice.

Adherents give special thought to their actions, as they believe that far-reaching consequences are transmitted through the wyrd. Heathens also recognize a particular obligation to family and friends, and place particular emphasis on honesty and hospitality.

The importance of righteous living in this world is stressed and little thought it given to any afterlife.

Valhalla – Odin's banqueting hall – is popularly seen as the Norse equivalent of heaven, but it is actually reserved for warriors who die in battle. Only half of them go there; the other half go to the meadow presided over by the goddess Freyja. Those who drown at sea are caught in the net of the goddess Ran, while people who die of natural causes go to the vast underworld mansion of the goddess Hel, where they are reunited with their ancestors.

Sources are too scant to enable a complete reconstruction of the pre-Christian idea of the soul. However, folk tales talk of the 'fylgia', or 'fetch', which is the part of the person which is manifest while living, but is not physically seen until just before death. In fact, Heathens believe that humans have four or five souls and the fetch is one of them. Only two of these souls survive the death of the body: one is the 'hugr' that goes to Valhalla or one of the other realms of the underworld, while the fetch goes through the process of reincarnation to be reborn as a new member of the original person's family or clan.

UNIVERSALISM VERSUS RACIALISM

Modern Heathenry has its origins in German Romanticism and the nationalist sentiment that led to the unification of Germany. A notable contribution to the ideals of German Romanticism was made by the Brothers Grimm via their collection of Germanic folk tales. The romantic movement stressed the idea of the 'volk' – the German-speaking people – and some proponents of it condemned Christianity as a Jewish invention. Many of these ideas were incorporated into Nazism, particularly by leading members of the Nazi Party such as Heinrich Himmler.

Among modern Heathens, there are 'folkish' groups whose

members believe that only those who are ethnically northern European can join, while other Heathens have a 'universalist' view and maintain that race is only a social construct. The folkish wing believes in the superiority of the biologically distinct Nordic, Aryan race, and some are explicitly white supremacists and separatists.

Heathens are generally socially conservative and put a premium on family values. While the more right-wing Heathens shun homosexuality, the percentage of lesbian, gay, bisexual and transgender members in Heathen groups more generally is high.

44

THE PALMARIAN
CATHOLIC CHURCH

On 30 March 1968 four schoolgirls aged between eleven and thirteen, known only as Ana, Josefa, Rafaela and Ana Maria, saw a figure picking flowers near a tree in an Alcaparrosan field in Andalusia. They later said they had seen 'the face of a very beautiful lady, with dark brown, beautiful eyes. At the beginning, we thought that it was a hangman or a bull with green horns, but later we saw that it was the face of a lady. It was very round and rosy, with a green thing around her head and she was dressed in a brown mantle. She smiled at us. It was the Virgin.'

While the girls said no more about the vision after their initial sighting, large crowds gathered in the Alcaparrosan field and pieces of the tree under which the girls had said they had seen the Virgin were made into a cross. Pilgrims took leaves and pieces of wood away as holy relics. Others who visited were said to fall into trances in which they saw the Virgin Mary, particularly if they were on top of a hill nearby that became known as Mount Christ the King. In these visions they were told that Mary and her son were crying over the destruction of the traditional faith. This was in light of changes introduced by the Second Vatican

Council, which aimed to bring the Catholic Church into line with the modern world.

Clemente Domínguez y Gómez, a twenty-two-year-old office clerk working on a Catholic journal, began visiting the site and on 15 August 1969 had a vision of his own. It was the first of many. Messages came to him from not only the Virgin Mary, but any number of saints and prophets, the 'Eternal Father' and Christ – often in the form of the 'Holy Face' which had been seen on the Turin Shroud. By 1975 Clemente Gómez had reported having had some sixty communications from divine sources. He gathered around him a group of followers who placed images of the Virgin Mary as the Divine Shepherdess and as Our Lady of Palmar at the site.

According to the heavenly messages, Gómez was charged with spreading devotion to the Holy Face throughout the world. His friend Manuel Alonso Corral, manager of a Catholic insurance firm who had lost his job after spending so much time at the site of the holy apparitions, typed up the messages Clemente had received and distributed them to pilgrims. Largely, these messages warned that it was the end time and that the faithful should pray and make reparation for the sins of humanity.

The Second Vatican Council had recommended that the mass be performed in the vernacular, but Gómez insisted that the Tridentine Mass in Latin must be reinstated. Gómez maintained that Pope Paul VI, who had brought about the modernization of services, had been drugged and held hostage by Masonic and communist curia, who had forced him into making modern statements. Gómez predicted that Paul VI would be succeeded by both the true pope and the antipope. By 1975, Gómez claimed he himself was the true successor.

To prove his point Gómez regularly exhibited the stigmata, the crucifixion wounds of Christ. Blood would gush from his forehead, hands, feet and side. On one occasion, witnesses testified he bled no less than 16 litres; the average human body contains between 4.5 and 5.5 litres of blood. A blanket stained by drops of his blood was cut up and distributed as relics.

The growing Palmarian Movement was supported by the Second Baroness of Castillo de Chirel, who, at the age of ninety, donated sixteen million pesos (over 200,000 euros) to the movement, although she later came to believe that Gómez and Alonso were fraudsters. They used the money to promote the Palmarian message worldwide and to buy the site of the original apparitions, upon which they built an elaborate shrine.

On the death of the Spanish dictator, Francisco Franco – who was later canonized by the Palmarian Church – Gómez founded the Order of the Carmelites of the Holy Face. To ordain priests and nuns in the order, they co-opted the Catholic Vietnamese Archbishop Pierre-Martin Ngô-dinh-Thuc, who was in exile in Italy after his brother, the South Vietnamese president Ngô-dinh-Diem, had been assassinated. He ordained Gómez and Alonso, who had not previously been part of the priesthood. The archbishop was promptly excommunicated by Rome.

Pope Paul VI was said to have been poisoned on 6 August 1978. The Palmarians maintained that the culprit was the Vatican's secretary of state, who was a Freemason of the highest degree, though no charges have resulted. Apparently, Christ appeared to Gómez and placed the papal tiara on his head. He was told he was to reign as Gregory XVII, calling himself the 'Great Pope of the End Times'. To legitimize his papacy, he created twenty-four cardinals, four of whom – including Alonso – placed the papal tiara on his head. Gregory XVII then declared popes John Paul I and later John Paul II to be antipopes and precursors of the Antichrist.

After the so-called Gregory XVII's death in 2005, Alonso succeeded him as pontiff of the Holy Catholic Apostolic Palmarian Church. He appointed himself as Peter II, and immediately canonized Gómez as Pope Saint Gregory XVII the Very Great. Pope Peter II was succeeded in 2011 by the Palmarian Church's secretary of state, who called himself Gregory VIII. Initially, Gregory VIII loosened the rules: previously, wearing jeans had been banned, women had not been allowed to wear trousers and followers were forbidden to talk to anyone who did not follow the strict dress code. The rules had forbidden swimming, trips to the beach, and even listening to music. Gregory VIII reversed the ban against these activities.

'Of course the ban on using the internet on mobiles, without express permission, continues,' Gregory VIII added.

Then it came to light that some two million euros' worth of donations might not have been declared to the tax office, although there was no further investigation. On top of allegations of tax evasion, the Palmerian Church was also said to have been involved in in laundering Mafia money. Gregory resigned in 2016 and went to live with his girlfriend, denying that he had stolen the two million euros, or the Palmarian pope-mobile: a top-of-the-range BMW. He also declared that the Palmarian Church had been a sham from the beginning and that published texts announcing the 'arrival of the Antichrist' in 2012 were 'lies'.

Nonetheless, he was succeeded by Pope Peter III, who said that his predecessor had fallen for an 'apostate woman'. He travelled to the US and Germany to rally the faithful, but many priests and nuns had left the movement. They were condemned in an apostolic letter, which said:

We, Peter III, hurl malediction against those perverse so-called 'Palmarian faithful', and may God's wrath fall upon them. And may they know that they are apostates, outside the true Church, in grievous sin against the Holy Ghost, and that they are committing terrible sacrileges. They are traitors, so many other Judas Iscariots. They deserve to be wiped off the face of the earth. God Himself will take charge. There is no lighting one candle to God and another to the devil.

Dan Brown, the author of *The Da Vinci Code*, used the Palmarian Catholic Church as a foil in his 2017 novel *Origin*, in which he erroneously stated that the church had canonized Adolf Hitler; however, it did make General Franco a saint.

MESSAGES FROM THE VIRGIN

In 1971 the Virgin Mary had apparently told Gómez: 'The Vatican is in the hands of Freemasons and Marxists. Freemasons and Pharisees have infiltrated the curia. They are the ones who obstruct the way of the Vicar of Christ. It is necessary to realize what will happen: there will be floods of blood on St Peter's Square. In this very moment, Communism and Freemasonry are preparing to make a decisive thrust and Marxism will usurp the church and sit on the throne.'

Moreover, after his assumption of the papacy in 1978, the Virgin purportedly told Gómez: 'My son: now you can see how rotten and corrupt the official church, the Roman Church is. Through her fornication, she has become the Great Whore. It is she who is in a pact with the enemies of Christ. It is she who respects all religions. It is she who preaches truths and lies at the same time. This Roman church is now nourished by a beast, the usurper John Paul II – the true church is no longer Roman. The true church is Palmarian, as you have preached yourself, assisted by the Holy Ghost. It is no longer possible to be Roman [Catholic], as the Holy See has been moved by the order of Christ.'

45

COLONIA DIGNIDAD

Bavaria in Latin America

olonia Dignidad – 'Dignity Colony' – was an agricultural colony of displaced Germans set up in southern Chile in the aftermath of the Second World War. In 1961 it was taken over by fugitive paedophile Paul Schäfer, who ruled the enclave with an iron first. Married couples were separated, their children taken away from them and sexually abused, but the sect escaped investigation for a long time because of its purported charitable status. During the military dictatorship of General Augusto Pinochet, it also served as a detention centre where opponents of the regime were tortured. It was also reportedly a haven for former Nazis. After the fall of Pinochet, Schäfer fled from Chile, only to be captured and jailed there for the rest of his life.

Paul Schäfer was born in Troisdorf, Germany, in 1921. He was a member of the Hitler Youth and served as a medic in the Luftwaffe during the Second World War. After the end of the war he ran an orphanage, but was forced to escape after being charged with sexually abusing boys in his care.

In 1961 he resurfaced at Colonia Dignidad, a utopian experiment which was set up in South America in the mid-1950s to promote and preserve German culture, language and education. Its residents wore traditional dress – lederhosen and dirndls – and lived in a Bavarian-style village, working in mills, factories, farms and the hospital that the community had built. Local Chileans were treated there for free, earning the inhabitants of Colonia Dignidad generous government subsidies.

Like other recruits, Helmut Schaffrick and his wife Emi had sold their house in Germany on the promise of a new life in Chile. They handed over the equivalent of 22,500 dollars to Schäfer, who told them that was enough for a temporary stay.

'But they were tricked,' said their son Horst. 'They thought they would build a place where they would do good works and live like good Christians. They found nothing but slavery and suffering.'

Some 300 people lived in the 70-square-mile enclave in the foothills of the Andes, surrounded by barbed wire, barricades, road blocks, searchlights, hidden cameras and microphones. Guard dogs were trained to hunt escapees and sensors were hidden under rocks surrounding the property.

Schäfer called himself *Der Permanente Onkel* ('The Permanent Uncle') to the inhabitants of Colonia Dignidad – and preached an apocalyptic creed to them which incorporated anti-semitism and anti-Communism. Former inmates said he was an unlikely-looking Messiah, with his long, grey hair and a glass eye, the result of an accident in his youth.

Occupants of the colony endured tough punishment, constant surveillance and brutal working conditions. Men were made to work in the mills and factories, women in the stables, kitchens and hospital. They sometimes worked for up to sixteen hours a day. Heinz Kunz, a former settler who left the group in the 1980s, said: 'I can't begin to tell you how hard he made me work ... twelve hours straight with nothing but bread or tea.'

People were subjected to beatings, electric-shock therapy and drugs. Youngsters were given sedatives to control them. After having a child, couples were then forced to live apart in single-sex dormitories and members were allowed few personal possessions. Newborn babies were taken from their mothers and raised by 'nurses' who were known as aunts. Once separated from their parents, Schäfer sexually abused the children. The community was totally isolated, with only a select few given access to news from the world outside.

Some people eventually managed to escape, bringing with them stories of the terrible conditions in the colony. But in 1973, a military coup brought General Pinochet to power in Chile. He needed places to house the left-wing opposition to his regime, many of whom would conveniently 'disappear' (and die). Schäfer cut Pinochet a deal. Some 350 people were tortured in a potato warehouse on the colony's grounds and about a hundred more were murdered and buried there.

In 1975 student activist Erick Zott Chuecas was arrested by the secret police and taken to the colony. He told the *Santiago Times*: 'They applied special bandages, putting wet cotton balls in my ears, putting a leather helmet over my head that covered my ears and tied my hands and feet. They didn't want me to know where I was being taken. When we entered the grounds of Colonia Dignidad, I had a feeling that this moment would be my last.'

His feet, legs and hands were bound and he was tied to a military camp bed. 'I was virtually immobilized,' he said. 'I was forbidden to speak and had no sense of time. They only took me out to interrogate and torture me ... then they tied me to a bed again. I would sleep from time to time and when I woke up I didn't know if I'd been asleep for ten minutes or two hours. Colonia Dignidad was a state within the Chilean state. It was hermetically sealed off from the outside world.'

It was so private that Pinochet and his inner circle of officers used it as a holiday destination. Nazi-hunter Simeon Wiesenthal said that Josef Mengele, the 'Angel of Death' who had experimented on inmates at Auschwitz, spent time there, while Walter Rauff, the SS's Obersturmbannführer who had invented the portable gas chamber, was known to have stayed in the area. Colonia Dignidad was purported to be a stronghold of former SS officers.

Meanwhile, the German embassy in Chile turned a blind eye to their activities in the country.

'For many years, from the 1960s to the 1980s, German diplomats looked the other way, and did too little to protect their citizens in this commune,' said German Foreign Minister Frank-Walter Steinmeier. 'Even later, when Colonia Dignidad was dissolved and the people were no longer subjected to the daily torture, the service lacked the determination and transparency to identify its responsibilities and to draw lessons from it.'

Pinochet stepped down as president of Chile in 1990, though he stayed on as Commander-in-chief of the Army until 1998. Meanwhile, Colonia Dignidad came under tentative investigation. After being charged with the sexual abuse of more than two dozen boys, Schäfer fled and was convicted of paedophilia in absentia. He was arrested in 2005 in Argentina and extradited back to Chile, where he was sentenced to twenty years for sexually abusing twenty-five children, while facing further charges which included kidnapping, forced labour, fraud and tax evasion.

He was also sentenced to three years for torture, seven years for homicide and three years for violating weapon control laws. A huge arsenal of weapons, comprising machine guns, grenades, surface-to-air missiles and Sarin nerve gas, was discovered at Colonia Dignidad. It had been stashed there by the Pinochet regime. In 2008 investigators found mass graves there. Then they unearthed cars buried there whose licence plates could be traced to missing political dissidents.

Schäfer died in 2010 at the age of eighty-eight, just five years into his sentence. Freed from his influence, Colonia Dignidad changed its name to Villa Baviera and has become a bizarre tourist destination which celebrates its German heritage. Bavarian music is piped from speakers. There are restaurants, and it can be rented out as a wedding venue. Many of the former inmates still live there as well, too institutionalized to leave.

THE COLONY

The 2015 movie *The Colony* tells the story of Lena and Daniel, a young couple who fall foul of the Chilean military coup in 1973. Daniel is abducted by Pinochet's secret police and Lena tracks him to a sealed-off area in the south of the country: Colonia Dignidad. The sinister colony presents itself as a charitable mission run by lay preacher Paul Schäfer and Lena decides to join the cult in order to try and find Daniel.

From his research, the film's director, Florian Gallenberger, said that Schäfer was a monstrous character: 'His abuse rate was unbelievable. He left Germany in 1951 but he had been abusing kids until the very last day he was in the country.' The residents of the colony were totally cut off from the outside world, he said. 'They didn't have radios, newspapers, even watches. There was only one rule and that was Paul Schäfer's rule and in the time he was in charge he developed a system whereby he could brainwash and torture the community more and more.'

Gallenberger visited the former site of Colonia Dignidad on several occasions during the making of the film. He even took the actress Emma Watson, who played Lena, there, and they went on a tour with a young resident.

'We were standing in what was then Paul Schäfer's bedroom,' Gallenberger said. 'They told us where the furniture was, and the bed, told us what Schäfer did. And it was very painful to hear. I asked what happened to the furniture. He hesitated for a moment, then said his parents were sleeping in it now. People had been abused in that bed for forty years and he said they were proud to be sleeping in it.'

It showed the level of brainwashing they had suffered.

'Their identity [was] crushed through forty years of isolation. There were some moments I couldn't believe what I was hearing – that really questioned what it meant to be human,' Gallenberger said.

46

OPUS DEI

God's Work

Opus Dei came to public attention as the sinister Catholic cult in Dan Brown's bestselling novel *The Da Vinci Code* and the subsequent film – although the cult has denied all charges Brown laid against it in his work. Founded in Spain in 1928 by Catholic priest Josemaría Escrivá de Balaguer and endorsed by the Vatican in 1950, it has since grown worldwide, accounting for roughly 83,000 lay members and 2,000 priests. Several million people around the world participate in its programmes and activities, which take place in more than sixty countries.

Born in Barbastro in northern Spain in 1902, Josemaría Escrivá was inexplicably cured of a grave illness at the age of two after doctors had given up hope. His parents took him to the nearby Shrine of Our Lady of Torreciudad in thanksgiving to the Virgin Mary, but misfortune continued to dog the family. In quick succession, his three sisters died at an early age, and his father's business failed.

At Christmas in 1917 he saw what he thought were the footprints of barefoot Carmelites in the snow, and took this as a sign that God was asking something of him. Two years later he began studying for the priesthood, entering the seminary at San Carlos in 1920. He was tonsured and received minor orders two years after that.

After his father died, Escrivá supported his family first as a deacon and then as a priest, but he later moved to Madrid to study law. Once there, he worked as chaplain to the Foundation for the Sick of the Apostolic Ladies of the Sacred Heart of Jesus. Then, on 2 October 1928, at a retreat, he suddenly saw what God had planned for him.

'I was twenty-six, had God's grace and good humour and nothing else. And I had to do Opus Dei,' he said. People, while pursuing their ordinary secular lives, could also do God's work. Ahead of his time, he soon realized that he could recruit women also to join Opus Dei.

During Spain's Second Republic, there were outbursts of anti-clerical violence. Nevertheless he managed to recruit Opus Dei's first members, particularly among university students, but as the danger grew he had to stop wearing priestly garb and go into hiding. Eventually, with other members, he crossed the Pyrenees on foot and found refuge in Andorra.

When he returned to Spain, he undertook pastoral work in Nationalist areas before spreading Opus Dei across the country. In 1943 he founded the Priestly Society of the Holy Cross, to allow Opus Dei to ordain priests. The first three were ordained the following year. The principal objective of the organization was to reach out to the laity: 'We have to be contemplative souls in the middle of the world, who strive to turn our work into prayer,' Escrivá said. 'Married people, single people, workers, intellectuals, farmers ... right where they are can and should be good children of God.'

Unlike other institutions within the Catholic Church, Opus Dei did not require followers to withdraw from the world. The idea was that members should engage with the world and bring spirituality into all aspects of their lives. Members were involved in running universities, university residences, schools, publishing houses, hospitals, and technical and agricultural training centres.

With the support of the Vatican, Opus Dei extended its mission worldwide. In 1950 Pius XII granted the Holy See's final approval to Opus Dei. In 1982 Escrivá became a personal prelate with direct responsibility to the pope and the order gained the right to train its own priests.

There are three types of Opus Dei members. The full members, who are called numeraries, make themselves available to work for the organization full-time; those in the women's branch are known as numerary assistants; and then there are the aggregated members or associates, who undertake one or more apostolic assignment, such as expanding the reach of the Church. Seventy per cent are known as extraordinary members or supernumeraries. They are the only ones who are allowed to marry.

While Opus Dei was on the side of the poor, sick and disadvantaged, it conscientiously avoided the political arena.

'There are no dogmas in temporal matters,' said Escrivá. 'If Opus Dei had been involved in politics, even for an instant, in that moment of error I would have left Opus Dei.' This was seen by some as disingenuous, as Opus Dei had sprung up under the Nationalist regime of General Franco and contributed several members to his government.

Maria del Carmen Tapia, author of *Beyond the Threshold: A Life in Opus Dei*, noticed how the writings of Escrivá flourished in the fertile soil of Franco's dictatorship after the Civil War. His first book, *Camino* (*The Path*), 'was a provocative invitation to post-war youth with practically no literature available other than religious books and the required textbooks approved by Franco's censorship,' she said. 'Father Escrivá offered the great adventure: to give up everything without getting anything in return; to conquer the world for Christ's church; a contemplative life through one's everyday work; to be missionaries, without being called such, but with a mission to accomplish. Students were challenged to excel in their chosen endeavour, turning study time into prayer, with the aim of attaining a high position in the intellectual world, and then offering it to Christ. It was not a question of becoming nuns or monks, but a real challenge to lay people who had never considered a religious vocation. Our apostolic field was our own environment, among our friends.'

Later she had her doubts, saying she had not 'see[n] the internal contradiction in this book where the frequent use of military language was combined with passages from the Gospel'. Over time, she came to see Opus Dei as a form of 'white freemasonry', noting how it plotted to 'capture' chairs (prestigious academic positions) at Madrid University, 'hoping to preserve them for members', and that it was 'ruthless about getting rid of anyone who was in their way'. She also said she heard 'stories of male members who courted young women, simply to recruit them for Opus Dei'.

After Escrivá's death in 1975, he was buried in the crypt of Our Lady of Peace, the Prelatic Church of Opus Dei in Rome. By then, Opus Dei was established in thirty-one different countries and had over 60,000 members, including over 1,000 priests. Escrivá was beatified in 1992 and canonized ten years later. Pope John Paul II called him the 'saint of the ordinary [people]'.

Of the organization, Pope John Paul II said: 'It has as its aim the sanctification of one's life, while remaining within the world at one's place of work and profession: to live the Gospel in the world, while living immersed in the world, but in order to transform it, and to redeem it with one's personal love for Christ. This is truly a great ideal, which right from the beginning has anticipated the theology of the lay state of the Second Vatican Council and the post-council period.'

THE DA VINCI CODE

Opus Dei responded to *The Da Vinci Code* by pointing out that the book and film were both works of fiction and not reliable sources of information. The novel's antagonist Silas was depicted as a monk, but, as they pointed out, Opus Dei was an institution for lay people and diocesan priests, not a monastic order. It had no monks. The order's numeraries did not take vows, wear robes, sleep on straw mats, nor spend all their time in prayer or corporal mortification. They went about their work in an everyday fashion.

'In fact, *The Da Vinci Code* gets Opus Dei's nature 180 degrees backwards,' Opus Dei's website said. 'Monastic orders are for people who have a vocation to seek holiness by withdrawing from the secular world; Opus Dei is for people who have a vocation to live their Christian faith in the middle of secular society.' Nor did they go about murdering, lying, drugging people and otherwise acting unethically, thinking that this behaviour would be justified for the sake of God, the Catholic church, or Opus Dei itself, it added.

'The Catholic Church teaches that one should never do evil, even for a good purpose,' their website said. Nor were they focused on gaining wealth and power, they added.

When it comes to practising mortification of the flesh, Opus Dei urges followers to make small sacrifices rather than extraordinary ones, in keeping with its spirit of integrating faith with secular life. 'Some Opus Dei members also make limited use of the cilice and discipline,' said the National Catholic News Service in 2006. (The cilice is the spiked garter which Silas wears in the film *The Da Vinci Code*.) '*The Da Vinci Code*'s description of the cilice and discipline is greatly exaggerated and distorted: it is simply not possible to injure oneself with them as the book and film depict.'

47

THE THULE SOCIETY

The Mystic Roots of the Nazi Party

Nazism itself could be described as a killer cult. It was certainly linked with a number of German mystical cults that took many of their ideas from the Rosicrucians and theosophists. One of them was led by an Austrian occultist named Guido von List, who had a huge cult following in Germany in the 1870s. He worshipped the Pagan god of war, Woden, or Odun, and one of the symbols he used in his ceremonies was the hooked cross, an ancient symbol of good fortune, otherwise known as the swastika. His cult spawned the Thule Society, which restricted its membership to high-ranking German Army officers and the professional classes.

Guido von List believed that there was a Jewish conspiracy against the so-called Aryan race, a theory he propounded before the First World War. One of his most dedicated disciples was a lapsed Cistercian monk called Adolf Lanz, who changed his name to Dr Jörg Lanz von Liebenfelds and went on to pioneer 'Ariosophy' (folk wisdom concerning the Aryan race) and to publish the magazine *Ostara*, which he subtitled as the 'Newsletter of the Blond and Masculists'.

Lanz von Liebenfelds founded the New Order of the Templars at the ramshackle Werfenstein Castle on the banks of the Danube. Upon the flagpole of the castle, he flew a flag with a swastika on it. One of his most fanatical followers was the young Adolf Hitler.

When the Nazi Party was in its infancy, Hitler decided that it should have a symbol to rival the Communist Party's hammer and sickle. Another occultist, Friedrich Kohn, came up with a suggestion. Kohn belonged to the German Order, a group underpinned by its occult practices who also believed in the supposed world-wide Jewish conspiracy. He believed that the only way to fight this conspiracy was for Nordic Freemasonry to respond in kind. Kohn suggested that the symbol should be a black swastika, symbolizing the triumph of Aryan will, on top of a white disc, symbolizing racial purity, with a red background, symbolizing blood. Hitler agreed, but in what has been interpreted as a gesture that goes some way towards being black magic, he reversed the swastika of the original Sanskrit icon. It was this swastika that became the emblem of the Nazi Party.

Another practitioner of the occult who was influential in the Third Reich was Karl Haushofer. Haushofer came from a military family and, after graduating from Munich University, he joined the German army. In the early years of the twentieth century he became interested in mysticism and travelled to India and the Far East. He became convinced that the Indo-Germanic people had originated in Central Asia and that it was they who gave nobility and greatness to the world. In Japan Haushofer joined a secret Buddhist cult. During the First World War, it was said that his ability to predict where shells would fall was uncanny and he was promoted to the rank of general.

After the war he returned to Munich University, where he began teaching his own theory, that of the 'Science of Geo-Politics'. This was thinly disguised nationalist propaganda. Haushofer promoted the idea that it was the destiny of the German people to rule Europe and Asia. The heartland of Central Asia was, of course, the Indo-Germanic people's ancient homeland and it had to be recovered from the Slavic peoples who now occupied it. It would be the centre of unassailable world power, he claimed. Haushofer ran a journal called the *Zeitschrift für Geopolitik* in which he expounded his views of Aryan superiority. He also said that on his travels he had discovered a race of supermen who lived in a vast cavern beneath the Himalayas at a place called Agharti. Similar ideas had been put forward by the Rosicrucians and by theosophists.

Thule was the northernmost land known to Greco-Roman geographers, and is probably the region we know as Scandinavia today. The Thule Society was set up in 1911 as a secret society set up to look into the mystical place of the birth of the Germanic people, which it identified as 'Ultima Thule', a lost landmass to the north of Iceland and Greenland. Members had to swear that they had no Jewish or 'coloured' blood in their veins.

One of Haushofer's students was Rudolf Hess. Hess became Haushofer's assistant before becoming Hitler's deputy in the Nazi Party. When Hess and Hitler were jailed for their failed putsch against the Bavarian government, Haushofer visited Hess in prison and that was where he met Hitler. He began visiting Hitler daily, and many of Haushofer's ideas were incorporated in *Mein Kampf*. Hess later said that Haushofer was the secret 'master magician' behind the Reich. His ideas of 'cones of power' were incorporated into the stagecraft of the Nuremberg rallies and he brought lamas from Tibet and members of the Green Dragon Society from Japan to Germany to lend the Nazi war effort their mystical backing.

In 1918 the Thule Society bought the newspaper *Münchener Beobachter* (*Munich Observer*), which, in their possession, became the *Völkischer Beobachter* (*People's Observer*) and the main Nazi newspaper. It was edited by Thule Society member Karl Harrer. Along with Anton Drexler, Harrer founded the Deutsche Arbeiterpartei – the DAP or German Workers' Party – in January 1919. That September, Adolf Hitler joined the Deutsche Arbeiterpartei and the following February he reformed it as the

Nationalsozialistische Deutsche Arbeiterpartei – the NSDAP or National Socialist German Workers' Party, also known as the Nazi Party.

Heinrich Himmler, head of the SS, was another believer in the occult. The SS used occult practices and worshipped the Nordic god Woden in ceremonies in a castle at Wewelsburg, in northwest Germany, where Himmler had built a temple known as the Hall of the Dead.

During the Second World War, such harmless practices as astrology and palmistry were banned in all German-occupied countries. Even occult organizations such as the Thule Society and the German Order, which had backed Hitler from the outset, were outlawed. Occult practice was confined to those at the top of the Nazi Party.

Whatever help the occult may have lent to Hitler, his evil experiment failed. But even in defeat, Hitler hung on to his beliefs. He delayed the day of his own suicide until the Pagan festival of Walpurgisnacht – the 'Night of the Witches' – killing himself on 30 April 1945.

THE AHNENERBE INSTITUTE

With the Thule Society outlawed, Himmler set up the Ahnenerbe Institute within the SS to continue the study of the 'ancient history' of the German people. It promoted some bizarre ideas. One was glacial cosmology: the idea that outer space was made of ice. This, Himmler believed, explained why Nordic men were superior – they had grown strong in snow and ice.

Glacial cosmology could also apparently explain the destruction of Atlantis. Another idea which emerged from the Ahnenerbe Institute was that the Aryans had come from Atlantis, but traces of their heritage could be found in twentieth-century Tibet. The Ahnenerbe Institute think tank also came up with the idea that Hinduism and Buddhism had Aryan origins. It is said that Himmler carried a copy of the Hindu scriptures around with him, the *Bhagavad Gita*, during the Holocaust, believing that somehow it relieved him of his guilt.

In 1938 Himmler sent an expedition to Tibet under SS officer Ernst Schäfer. One of its objectives seems to have been to prove that the Aryan people had migrated from Tibet to Europe fifteen centuries earlier. Cranial measures and facial casts were taken of local people. The expedition also returned with ancient Tibetan texts which were said to have been of Aryan origin.

In June 1941 the Institute commandeered the 900-year-old Bayeux Tapestry in a bid to decode its Nordic symbolism as, in their eyes, it showed the Germanic Franks overwhelming their English enemies. There were also plans to make expeditions to Bolivia, Iran and Iceland to examine the inscriptions, customs and folklore of these countries, and also one to the Canary Islands, where there were mummies that they believed might illuminate the Aryan past. But the Institute's main project was the Aryanization of the Nazis' conquered territories in Eastern Europe, which Himmler estimated would take twenty years.

48

THE YAZIDI

The World's Oldest Religion?

The Yazidi were thrust into the international limelight in August 2014 when they were surrounded and butchered by the jihadis of the Islamic State, who characterized them as 'devil worshippers'. The Yazidi see themselves as 'worshippers of God', and their religion reveres both the Koran and the Bible. It also has links to Zoroastrianism and even sun worship. Their shrines are often decorated with depictions of the sun and their graves point east, towards the rising sun. Fleeing the Islamic State's jihadis, they took refuge on Mount Sinjar. Men who refused to convert to Islamic fundamentalism were murdered or worked to death. Women were raped or taken as sex slaves.

Traditionally, the Yazidi lived in small communities scattered across north-west Iraq, north-west Syria and south-east Turkey. Before the recent persecution, there were probably fewer than 100,000 followers. Their origins are unclear, but their calendar stretches back over six millennia; their Year One is 4,570 BC on the Christian calendar.

The Yazidi believe that they were created separately from the rest of mankind and so keep themselves strictly segregated from those who live around them. Any Yazidi who marries out of the group is considered to have taken on the religion of their spouse and is no longer permitted to call himself or herself Yazidi.

They are monotheists, believing in one creator God known as Yasdan. However, he is a remote entity and so the world is left in the care of seven holy beings, or angels. Chief among them is Tawsi Melek, the Peacock Angel. The peacock is a symbol of immortality for the Yazidi, because its flesh does not appear to decay.

The Yazidi reject the idea of evil, sin, the devil and hell. According to their religion, the fallen angel repented of the sin of pride before God and was pardoned and returned to his position of the chief of the angels. This has led others to believe that the Yazidi worshipped the devil.

The Yazidi pray five times a day to Tawsi Melek (they consider Yasdan too elevated to pray to). The other name of the deity Tawsi Melek is Shaytan, which is the Arabic for devil. The Yazidis believe in reincarnation: souls pass into successive bodily forms, being gradually purified through continual rebirth, which makes any concept of hell unnecessary.

Sunni Muslim extremists, such as those of the Islamic State, believe that the Yazidis' name derives from Yazid ibn Muawiya, who was the deeply unpopular second caliph of the Umayyad dynasty and whose suppression of a rebellion made the split between Sunni and Shia Muslims permanent. Modern research, however, has clarified that the Yazidis' name has nothing to do with Yazid, but is taken from the modern Persian 'ized', which means angel or deity. The name Izidis simply means 'worshippers of God', which is how the Yazidis describe themselves. Their own name for themselves is Daasin (plural: Dawaaseen), which is taken from the name of an old Nestorian diocese, the Ancient Church of the East named after the Christians.

The Yazidi believe that Sheikh Adi ibn Musafir, a Sufi Muslim who died in 1162, is an avatar of Tawsi Melek. His tomb in the village of Lalish, some 60 kilometres north of Mosul, in Iraq, is the centre of their annual pilgrimage, which takes place between 15 and 20 September. There are two sacred springs there and pilgrims perform ritual ablutions in the river.

Lalish is also supposed to have been the place where Tawsi Melek descended to earth. He had been sent by Yasdan to stop the earth shaking after an earthquake. Once there, the seven colours of his plumage were transformed into a rich abundance of flora and fauna. He is believed to have then travelled to the Garden of Eden, where he breathed life into Adam, thereby endowing him with a soul. Turning Adam towards the sun, the symbol of the creator, Tawsi Melek taught him a daily prayer, repeating it in seventy-two languages for the sake of the seventy-two tribes who would eventually inhabit the earth.

Eve was then created. But, apparently, before Adam and Eve could copulate, Tawsi Melek held a competition to see whether either of them could reproduce on their own. He took their reproductive juices and sealed them in jars. When Eve's was opened, it was filled with insects and vermin, but Adam's jar contained a beautiful boy child known as Shedid bin Har, or Son of Jar. He was the father of the Yazidi and passed down his wisdom to his people.

Humankind was then purified by a series of floods. The last occurred around 6,000 years ago, and that was when the Yazidi religion crystallized. Their religion was reformed in the eleventh century AD by Sheik Adi, who wrote the *Book of Revelation* which forms Yazidi scripture.

In the *Book of Revelation* God says: 'I was, am now, and shall have no end. I exercise dominion over all creatures and over the affairs of all who are under the protection of my image. I am ever present to help all who trust in me and call upon me in time of need. There is no place in the universe that knows not my presence.'

GENOCIDE OF THE YAZIDI

The Yazidi are the caretakers of the oldest religious tradition on earth. They are a peaceful people, but over the last 700 years it is estimated that twenty-three million of them have been killed by Sunni Muslim extremists. Two hundred years ago there were two million Yazidi; now there are fewer than one million worldwide. The worst persecution in recent history took place under the jihadis of the Islamic State.

On 3 August 2014 the Islamic State's fighters attacked their villages, killing at least 5,000 Yazidi men and kidnapping over 7,000 Yazidi women. Thousands fled and found refuge on Iraq's desolate Mount Sinjar, awaiting military assistance from the US and its allies. Thousands of Yazidis escaped during the ensuing bombing raids, but many were forced to remain. Those who survived could not return home and ended up in refugee camps across the Syrian border.

Seven years before that, Kurdish Sunni Muslim extremists set off four truck bombs in the Yazidi town of Sinjar, where 500 Yazidis were killed and 200 gravely injured. Earlier on, Saddam Hussein had sought to wipe them out completely, destroying some 250 Yazidi villages around Mosul and in the Sinjar mountains. The River Dejeula which supplied Yazidi communities with drinking water was poisoned and their sacred sites were vandalized.

Half a million Yazidis still live in Iraq, 10,000 in Syria, 5,000 in Turkey, and some 190,000 in Germany. There are also large Yazidi communities in Russia, Belgium, Armenia, Georgia, France and Sweden. Since the 1990s, small communities have also been established in the United States.